The
Ultimate Goal!

*Allen Carmichael, as the adaptor of this book,
would like to record his particular thanks
to the following people and organisations
for their help in providing information,
statistics, advice and support:*

The Direct Sales Association
The Direct Mail Information Service
Towers Perrin

...and by no means least!
S.M.P
Bill & Jeanne Quain
Wales Publishing Company

The
<u>ULTIMATE</u>
<u>GOAL!</u>

...mapping the route to Financial Freedom

A British adaptation
by
ALLEN CARMICHAEL

of the original
American best-selling book
'Reclaiming the American Dream'
by
BILL QUAIN Ph.D

CONCEPT

Other books by Allen Carmichael:

"MULTI-LEVEL MARKETING"

ISBN 1 873288 00 X   *Concept* - July 1990

"NETWORK & MULTI-LEVEL MARKETING" (retitled 2nd edition)

ISBN 1 873288 01 8   *Concept* - September 1991, Reprinted - June 1993, April 1994

Revised 3rd edition. October 1995 (ISBN 1 873288 14 X)

"THE NETWORK MARKETING SELF-STARTER"

ISBN 1 873288 02 6

Concept - November 1991 2nd edition - August 1994 (ISBN 1 873288 09 3)

"BELIEVE YOU CAN!"

ISBN 1 873288 03 4   *Concept* November 1992

"FOUR-SQUARE-SELLING"

ISBN 1 873288 04 2 *Concept* November 1994

'THE ULTIMATE GOAL!' © *Concept* & *Wales Publishing Company, USA.* 1995

ISBN 1 873288 19 0   *Concept* - October 1995

A British adaptation of 'Reclaiming the American Dream' (ISBN 0-9623646-1-4)

© *Wales Publishing Company - USA 1994*

P.O.Box 1146. North Wales. PA 19454. USA

Book and cover designed by Allen Carmichael

Printed in Finland by Werner Soderstrom Osakeyhitio

Published by *CONCEPT* . PO Box 614 . Polegate . East Sussex . BN26 5SS . England

Telephone/Fax: 01323 485434

Contents

The original introduction to
Reclaiming The American Dream
By Bill Quain Ph.D

'What is the highest salary I can expect from a job?'
The question came from a young woman seated in my office
at the university where I teach in the business school.   She
was serious.   I was appalled.
She was a 21 year old, smart, responsible, energetic and
popular individual, with excellent leadership potential.   Yet
she wanted to know what someone else would allow her to
earn.

❖*She wanted me, and her future employer, to tell her
what she could expect the limits of her own potential would
be!   Where had we gone wrong?*

She is typical of the majority of people.   She is one of us.

I found myself thinking, *'what can people do to break the
bonds that limit our ability to create wealth?   What can I tell
these students about opportunity, freedom and self
determination?'*

MY LIFE - MY CHOICES
When I was 21, I didn't know much - but I did know that
working for someone else was not for me.   By that time I had
already successfully owned and operated two businesses.   At
the age of 19, I had a hotel in a resort area.   It was hard
work, but the rewards were equal to the effort.

I discovered very early in life that this country(*the USA*)
offered each person a great gift.   The gift is FREE
ENTERPRISE.   Anyone, I mean anyone, can own their own

business, set their own goals and achieve whatever they want - without limits! *What a revelation!*

My friends made different choices. They took jobs and were told how much they would make.

It didn't matter how hard they worked, they would still be paid the same hourly rate. Many of them are still facing limits to their earning potential. Although, now it is even more restrictive. Now they are on salaries. So, even if they work more hours, they still make the same amount.

And who determines the amount they make? It doesn't matter, because if *someone else* determines their salary, their potential, then they will always be under rewarded.

Throughout my life I have tried to make choices that would not limit my potential. Yes, I am a full-time professor, but I also am a speaker, writer and small business owner. I always want to be in a position that allows me the freedom to reach the greatest potential for which I am capable. The only way to do that is to participate in the free enterprise opportunity of business ownership.

A LONG SEARCH

Even though I wanted no part of a system that meant virtual slavery to bosses, restrictive policies and salary caps, I had not found a solution that could be offered to others. After all, traditional business ownership requires vast star-up capital, overwhelming government interference, and the costs of inventory, employees and buildings. And there is the issue of time.

Who has the capital and time to invest in their own business? Certainly my students did not. Neither did most of the participants in the training sessions and seminars I provided.

Yet I knew that people were becoming wealthy. I could see it. Where did they get their money? How did they achieve their lifestyles?

I decided to find out. I owed it to my students, my friends and myself. I began in the 'normal' places, looking at the corporate and professional worlds. The answer wasn't there.

❖ *Finally, I found it. A system that was so simple, yet vastly effective, that the potential was literally unlimited. I knew I had to study it, to examine it. If it met the claims of those who were already making a fantastic living in this system, I knew I would write a book about it. Obviously, this system has made it!*

TAKE MY ADVICE - OR NOT!

After carefully reviewing, analyzing and observing this system, I am able to recommend it to anyone with the desire to attain financial freedom. It is foolproof!

But, everyone must make their own decisions. While the business does not require money, it does demand self-control, commitment and motivation.

You will find the answers to four questions in this book:
1. Why do you need a free enterprise based business of your own?
2. What is this business?
3. What will you be doing?
4. Will it work for you?

SO WHAT DO I TELL MY STUDENTS?

Remember the young lady that I mentioned at the beginning of this book? What should I tell her, and others like her?

Now I tell them that there are alternatives. They do not have to resign themselves to a life of salary caps, downsizing and layoffs. I can tell them that free enterprise is alive and well.

❖ *My advice to them, and to you, is to dare to be different.*
Look for possibilities, not restraints.
Find a reliable system with a proven track record.
Make the most of opportunities by examining each one with an open mind.
Use the free enterprise system and live life as an entrepreneur.
In short, RECLAIM THE AMERICAN DREAM!

Bill Quain - 1994

Introduction to
'The Ultimate Goal!'

Some time ago I was approached by an American friend , an entrepreneur engaged, most successfully, in the free enterprise system that is the subject of this book - and given a copy of Bill Quain's original American publication, *'Reclaiming The American Dream'*. He said he felt I should read the book with a view to a possible British adaptation of its vibrant message.

Bill's book greatly impressed me with its carefully argued, yet relentlessly pursued investigation of all the facts that lead to an indisputable conclusion - the system about which he writes really works and has brought financial freedom to tens of thousands of people, not just in the United States, but all over the world.   Why was I approached? Simply because I had already written two books on the subject of this free enterprise system.

In 1990, like so many other people, I was made redundant. Not fun!   I have written several articles on the subject of redundancy, and the devastating effects it can have.   I have also written a book on the psychology of self-belief, success and achievement, that was really sparked off by my own experience.

It was whilst I was casting about, with the idea of starting a new career (I have already had several others) as a writer, that I first encountered the system which is the subject of this book.   I was totally fascinated by the concept.   I soon discovered that there was no British book on the subject, so it was only a small stride that took me to the idea that *I would write that book!*

The resultant small volume became internationally accepted as the most concise introduction to the subject, and has been adopted, virtually, by a whole industry. I can certainly claim to have been responsible for introducing thousands of people to a business opportunity that has altered their lives beyond all recognition.

Those, then, are my credentials.

But why a British adaptation of an existing American book? *The American Dream* is something we, in this country, have always known about, yet have nothing that quite matches it as a universal concept for the freedom of entrepreneurial self development and general financial advancement through ambition. So, the title, *Reclaiming The American Dream* might not have the immediate appeal in this country that it deserves. A certain amount of the original book's content is what we might regard as *very American.* That is not meant as derogatory in any way - it is a simple statement of fact.

In writing *The Ultimate Goal!* my aim has been to produce an Anglicised version of Bill Quain's book, without loosing any of its fascinating message. If it can be as instrumental as its American original in pointing out *the route to financial freedom,* what more could we ask?

There are many, many people in Britain to whom the message contained in this book could make a significant difference. It might even mark a turning point in their fortunes. I sincerely hope that *The Ultimate Goal!* can play a part in helping to produce those *green shoots of recovery* we used to be told about. I am delighted to have formed the valuable relationship with Bill Quain that has developed, like a technological ping-pong match of faxes and phone calls, across the Atlantic.

Allen Carmichael - November 1995

Part One

THE SEARCH IS ON...

Chapter One
What's in it for me?

You have just opened a book that holds the possibility of completely changing your life.   That at least was the original intention in writing it. - *to produce a book that would have the ability to awaken you to the potential of a system that is proving to be the most significant economic transition of this generation.*

The immediate question that may spring into your mind is
'OK! but what's in it for me?'
The answer to that is simple...

❖ *Any ambitious individual now has the opportunity within his or her grasp for increased wealth and personal growth.*

FREEDOM AND CHOICE
Most people find it difficult to accept the idea that they could be totally financially free and independent.   Free from debt and free from any sort of financial worry or, indeed, control by others.   Just imagine the feeling!

This freedom, in the United States, is what has always been known as *The American Dream* - but a great many people would consider it out of reach today.

Nothing could be further from the truth!

Let's define *financial freedom.*   What would it actually mean to you - and what would it mean to your family?   In a nutshell,   it would mean *absolute freedom to pursue the*

15

things in life that are the most important to you. That surely could be deemed to be success - and one definition of the word is *'to be able to spend your life in your own way'.*

Being free means having choices - the choice to do whatever *you* want to do, the choice to go to work or not. The freedom of choice as to which partner stays at home to take care of the family. And what about holidays? Are these a regular feature in your life? How many times a year are you able to get away and enjoy a complete break? How often have you felt that you can't afford a real family holiday? It would be wonderful to get away with the children, but the sheer expense usually kills the possibility stone dead. Have you ever thought what fun it would be to simply dash off on the spur of the moment to some fascinating European capital for a weekend? But the thing that stops you may not just be the expense of such a trip - it is the added expense of having to get someone to look after the children. It all becomes too much, and so, like so many things in life, it just does not happen.

But - and think carefully about this - if you had *financial freedom*, all these choices would be a part of that freedom. So ask yourself the simple question...*'do I have all the freedom of choice that I would like?'* Only you can provide the answer to that...

A SYSTEM AND A MENTOR

A mentor is a teacher. A mentor is a person for whom you have respect, someone you perceive as already successful. We have all known such role models in our lives - people that we respected and admired. We saw something in them that we would have liked to see in ourselves. For this reason, we did what they did, in the belief that something approximating to their success would rub off on us. Imagine what it would mean to you to find a *system*, and with it *an unlimited supply of mentors* to help and guide you towards wealth and financial freedom.

❖ *Imagine these mentors - all successful entrepreneurs - showing you and others a system that would bring unlimited success, mentors that want you to succeed. This is what, in the United States is known as a win-win situation!*

And that is only the starting point, for, as you grow, you will become a mentor to others, in turn helping *them* to succeed.   And what will be the affect of that on you?

❖ *You will experience astonishing personal growth. You will become a better listener and a greater leader.   You will develop great friendships - but,   above all...you will become wealthy!*

That is what's in it for you.

WHO WILL PAY MY BILLS?

Whatever your particular dream, maybe the shadows cast by the huge corporate clouds across our economic landscape, make it difficult to believe that the fulfilment of such dreams is possible.   Most people are too worried about tomorrow, about job security and paying the mortgage.   The burden that the current recession has placed on many people will take a long time to remove.   It needs more than casual remarks about *'the green shoots of recovery'* to convince people that a better future is about to dawn.   Many people have suffered redundancy, job loss, or the collapse of a small business that may have taken years to build.

Being short of cash is certainly not fun, and certainly not a recent trend either. There always seems to be more month than money. But things do *not* have to be like that! The *opportunity* and the *system* are already in place that could alter things significantly, making it possible for you to pay the mortgage *and* save a modest amount each month, to have regular holidays with the children *and* to take those occasional breaks on your own. Clearly if these things are possible, your life must change dramatically - but, how can this be achieved? To change the circumstances that surround you, *you* must change - and that is not as difficult as you might imagine.

All that is needed is *desire and commitment.*

The systems and the mentors are already there, at this very moment, creating the solution. It is your *desire* to see your life change, followed by the *commitment* to follow the path that is unfolding that will bring about the realisation of all your dreams.

AN INCOME FOR LIFE - AND BEYOND...

At present you are probably either salaried or a wage-earner. The entrepreneurial business opportunity we are discussing, developed over the past 30 years, offers residual income - and that is a very different proposition, in income terms, to either salaries or wages.

❖*A residual income provides you and your heirs with a steady, dependable cash flow, even if you were unable to work. This is a situation infinitely better than having money in the bank and living off the interest.*

All this is possible because of a dramatically new business concept. You are probably used to selling your time for money, being paid what the job is worth. In the business we are talking about *you are paid what you are worth!* You are rewarded for effort. You are looking at profit sharing and other incentives. This is free enterprise at its very best!

You will be the owner of your own business, without the financial risks that usually go with new ventures. You will be inspired, motivated and helped. Your overheads will be minimal and your capital commitment negligible.

Does it sound too good to be true?

'Too good to be true' is often the reason for not taking something seriously, and for not taking action - so, please, do not be put off by such thoughts.

❖ *Success will not come overnight. It will only take a few years of dedicated work - but the reward is...*

TOTAL FREEDOM!

WEALTH BY ASSOCIATION

Look around you. Are you surrounding yourself with positive influences? Do you see yourself as a positive influence on others?

❖ *The only way to succeed - the ONLY way - is to live a positive life, surrounded by positive, successful people.*

The choice, as always, is yours. You can choose to be like everyone else and remain a prisoner, a slave to employers and others who control your life. Or, you can decide that it doesn't have to be like that. You can seek out the people who have already broken out of the circle and have achieved their own independence.

What's in it for you? You will become like the people you admire. They will teach you, and you, in your turn, will teach others. You will be an active, committed contributor to your own future and fortune.

WHAT IS *WEALTH?*

Everyone must decide what the answer is to this question for themselves. Wealth is a purely relative state. To some it may be no more than balancing the books each month, but to others it could be much, much more.

Wealth is freedom. Wealth is personal development. It is the opportunity to share, to give and to receive. It is a total picture embracing family, friends and a total lifestyle.

You can have wealth. You can grow, prosper and achieve. Becoming an entrepreneur can provide you with tangible rewards as well as recognition, status, fulfilment and love.

You can take pride and satisfaction in helping others towards their own achievement. True success will be built and modelled on the success of others through the sharing of a commitment to worthwhile ideals. Wealth is not *just* the achievement of financial rewards - it is an amalgam of all we have talked about.

❖ *So that's what's in it for you!*
This entrepreneurial, win-win, mentor system is outpacing the traditionally structured, less effective corporate world. The path to wealth is awaiting you. All it requires is that you apply the ingredients of enthusiasm, determination and

belief in your own abilities. In doing this, you will have the energy to overcome all the obstacles - and your reward will be to set yourself totally free.

Chapter Two
A business revolution
- the return to ownership

This chapter briefly traces the development of business trends in America. In Britain it has always been said that when the Stock Market sneezes in America, handkerchiefs come out in London! American trends are of particular interest since, with only a slight time-lapse, patterns will most likely be repeated here.

We will examine the cycle of business ownership and entrepreneurial free enterprise. You will see how the American economy - built on the principles of free enterprise - is once again offering individuals an outstanding opportunity to take charge of their lives, secure their financial futures, and live as free men and women.

The economic forces that shape our daily lives are changing rapidly due to the massive improvements and innovations in new technology. Our world is shrinking as we become exposed to the ideas, dreams, hopes and innovations offered by people from around the globe. But few Americans have utilised the economic opportunities offered by globalisation to improve their own lives.

❖ *Each individual must prepare to face the challenges and seize the opportunities offered by the swiftly changing technological and economic situation.*

FREE ENTERPRISE IN AMERICA

The U.S. economy was originally based on a concept of entrepreneurs working together to create free enterprise and free capitalism. The merchant class - the entrepreneurs of today - was the backbone of the American revolution. These individuals were unwilling to bear the tyranny of a system that placed class structure and government interference above the dreams of the individual. The American economy was founded on the principle that each person had the right to pursue their own financial dreams.

The founders of the United States had very strong economic as well as political views. Their economic values were best reflected in the writings of Adam Smith, a noted Scottish economist of the day. His powerful economic credo, defined in his epic work *The Wealth of Nations* (published in 1776, the same year as the Declaration of Independence), declared that all men should be allowed to seek the benefits of free enterprise through their own hard work.

THE RISE OF THE ENTREPRENEUR

Business flourished in post revolutionary America, built upon the endeavours of the individual. Inventors brought great innovations to the marketplace. American entrepreneurs seized these technologies and put them to work.

As immigrants swarmed to American shores, they carried with them a dream - to own a business of their own, to have land, and to secure a place in society for their family. Most of all they saw opportunity.

❖ *They did not fear work. They only feared a lack of opportunity.*

24

THE INDUSTRIAL REVOLUTION

The Industrial Revolution was a time of vast economic and social change. Great factories sprang up using the new technologies. Workers were needed to produce the standardised goods that were now so popular. The great waves of immigrants were funnelled into foundries, factories and plants. *The American Dream* turned from self ownership to full employment.

It is this legacy of trading time for money that is such a strong part of the American system today. Unfortunately, it is also one of the primary causes for the weakening of the social fabric.

Of course the industrial revolution did spur a continued increase in the standard of living. Machines and new technologies made life easier. But it was the leaders of the industrial revolution, not the great numbers of workers, who grew wealthy. These entrepreneurs learned to combine the work of many people with improving technology to reap outstanding incomes.

One of the major reasons that the industrial revolution was so prominent and successful is that it reduced costs. According to the economist, Paul Zane Pilzer, at the time of the industrial revolution, the cost of goods that appeared on the store shelf was 85% for manufacture and 15% for distribution. Any new technology that could reduce manufacturing costs led to huge profits. The leading entrepreneurs of the industrial revolution were the technicians who were able to reduce those costs. A prime example was Henry Ford.

❖ *Today, cost structures are vastly different.*
Only 15% of the cost of most goods are attributable to
manufacturing. 85% of the costs of goods on retail shelves
are distribution. This is an important premise for the
entrepreneurs of today who wish to seize opportunities.

POST WORLD WAR II

The mobilisation of the American industrial complex helped the U.S. emerge from the war as the leading economic world power. While the rest of the world was rebuilding from the carnage, U.S. factories were in full production. Returning servicemen were eager to reclaim their jobs and forge a new future. They wanted the sacrifices they made to become the foundation for a new land - bright with *The American Dream.*

And the post war years seemed to have it all. *The American Dream* had now firmly shifted from business ownership to a new model. Veterans used the G.I.Bill to attend college in record numbers. Men who had learned to fight and win a war by working in the rigid military structure were now applying the same theory to their corporate structures.

The American Dream could now be summed up as - *Get a good education, get a good job, save money, buy a home, retire and be happy* - and for the next two and a half decades, this was a plausible dream.

THE RISE OF THE CORPORATION

Huge corporations became the most significant and visible sign of economic security. Layer upon layer of workers, supervisors, middle managers and executives were formed.

A man or woman could work their whole lives for a single corporate giant.

New technologies were again creating opportunities for corporations. The massive amount of capital needed to enter new markets precluded individuals from gaining power. The cost of distribution was staggering. It required the resources of a huge conglomerate to produce goods and then put them into the hands of the consumer.

The structures created in this era became the great force in the land, and leaders of this corporate revolution, the great moguls of industry, ruled with almost limitless power, because they, and only they, could move goods from factory to consumer, and because they had the only access to information.

THE PROBLEM WITH THE CORPORATE WORLD

There were outstanding factors that contributed to corporate America's downfall, one of which was an inability to react to global competition.

Consider the car industry. American cars have improved greatly in quality - but only because the Japanese were stealing the market by creating exceptional service and dependability. It took American industry many years to wake up to what was happening. Now, much of the damage has been done. Hundreds of thousands of Americans have lost their jobs - *and they will never get them back!*

A second problem, the lack of incentives, is perhaps even more devastating. The structure of the corporate world has almost eliminated the motivation of the average worker and executive to create improved service and quality. The reason is very simple. *You will scarcely ever be allowed to make all the money you want.*

❖ *Think about it!*
Has anyone ever sat down and asked you what you want?
Has anyone ever said ' we are concerned about you and we
want to make sure that you can make all the money you
need to reach your dreams'?
Probably not...

Remember this - if you want to create security, wealth and financial freedom, *it will never happen if you work for someone else.*

GLOBAL COMPETITION

Global competition is a direct result of the technologies that have made it possible to cross borders electronically. Even relatively poor countries can now acquire the technology necessary to compete on a world basis. And this trend directly affects the job security of, not only Americans, but the British too.

In response to the influx of global competitors, the corporations of America have begun to create leaner, meaner corporate staffs. This means, in the long term, redundancies and layoffs.

❖ *Global competition is a term to which we never paid*
much attention - and now it is threatening YOUR security.
YOU could be laid off to better enable your company
to compete with the rest of the world!

Both here and in America, everyone knows someone who has been made redundant or forced into early retirement. It is a fact that, in Britain since 1990, five million people have lost their jobs. Perhaps you have suffered redundancy yourself.

Most people blame it on the recession of the early 90's. If that was the case, those jobs would be reinstated as soon as the down-turn was over. Do you think those jobs are coming back? Not a chance!

Almost every American corporation, just as almost every British company, has made dramatic cuts in staff levels, often disguised, in some odd attempt to lessen the blow, by the use of such contrived titles as *de-hiring, accelerated retirement, contractural disengagement, stimulated second opportunity* or simply *outplacement.* If you were you one of the unfortunate souls that suffered redundancy or was pushed into early retirement, I am certain you got no comfort from the name in which it was wrapped. If you are one of the lucky ones - one of those who was not cast aside - do you really feel you have job security? Or do you worry about when your company will apply the squeeze?

In Britain in 1989, 6.2% of the potential total workforce was unemployed. By 1993 that figure had slowly but relentlessly risen to 10.3%.

GLOBALISATION AND YOU

The average person does not picture themselves as a global force, and yet the individual is said to be at the centre of power. John Naisbitt, author of *'The Global Paradox',* states that, *'while the changes in technology now offer large corporations the ability to compete globally, these same advances give individuals tremendous power - the power of information and networking.'*

Globalisation has only been made possible through communications technology - and this is something that is available to almost anyone. Nobody can deny the value of computers, voice mail, fax machines, networks, etc.

❖ *For a very small investment, individual entrepreneurs can develop a home-based office that can tap into the communications power of a world-wide network. This is the trend that can set you free financially!*

Over 200 years ago Adam Smith predicted that entrepreneurs would work together in networks to create a powerful free enterprise system. He could not have imagined the technological revolution.

His basic idea is alive and thriving today!

You do not have to be a computer buff to take advantage of the new opportunities. In fact, you do not even need to own or operate any of this equipment. You need only to be willing to work hard and associate with the entrepreneurs who have already put this technology network into action.

FRANCHISING

Franchises take advantage of communications technology and focus on standardisation. They began to expand in the 1970's, and today they are a familiar fixture on the business scene.

Franchises offer several advantages. Firstly they reduce risk. By following an established business system, entrepreneurs can increase their chances of business survival, and, once a system has been developed, it can be taught to others. A franchise is, in fact, a network of professionals - surely Adam Smith would have approved.

Franchises also offer individual ownership, and franchisees have virtually no limits to their potential income. If they work hard, follow the laid-down system and stick to the working plan, they can become wealthy.

30

There are, however, several distinct disadvantages to franchising. The financial outlay can be huge, involving buildings, inventory, maintenance and many other considerations.

Most franchises require the operation of a traditional business. The franchisee must hire managers to be present during all working hours, and the number of employees needed to run a successful, traditional business can be a real headache, not to mention the problem and difficulty of motivating, possibly unwilling people, to constantly do a good job.

A franchiser once told Bill Quain...*'many people just end up buying a job rather than owning a business.'* Rather than buying the freedom they hoped for, they simply buy another gruelling place of employment.

❖ *But, what if there was a system that had the advantages of franchising - business ownership, professional networking and assistance, without the disadvantages? Wouldn't that be terrific? Imagine, limitless potential with no inventory, no employees and no capital requirements.*

THE GREATEST BUSINESS OPPORTUNITY IN YOUR LIFETIME

Where will you be five years from now?
Will you still be watching the world go by?

❖ *The question is - 'Will you believe your own instincts?' You know that your financial future is at risk. Now all you have to do is take advantage of the economic opportunities and GO!*

Consider these two important facts:

1. Distribution - bringing goods and services from the producers to the consumers - represents 85% of the costs of doing business.

2. Technology has made it possible for individuals - that is ordinary people - to work together to take advantage of the changing economy...*and to make fortunes!*

If you could use a network of entrepreneurs to tap into the riches offered by reducing distribution costs, *would you be interested?*

And if the money it took to get involved was no more than the average weekly pay packet, *would you be interested?*

And if you were given assistance by people who had already become rich. free and independent, *would that make it even more interesting?* It certainly should!

ENTER NETWORKING

In the 1950's when franchising was in its infancy, another financial movement began to take hold in the USA. It was developed to bring consumers and producers together, thus reducing distribution costs.

Network Marketing was similar to Adam Smith's concept of free enterprise, but with several improvements. Unlike that great amorphous mass, the corporate world, Network Marketing has unlimited potential for the individual. Unlike franchising, the costs of entry are minimal, and most distributors have neither overheads, inventory nor employees. And with the technological revolution, network marketers can easily become involved in a system that makes managing their business easy and efficient.

After only a few years and an unfortunate false start which was known as *Pyramid Selling*, Network Marketing, or as it was more widely called in the early years, *MLM*, arrived in Britain and took up residence here.

Many large corporations and organisations in both the USA and Britain were quick to recognise the benefits of direct distribution, creating network companies of their own. Other companies, seeing the same opportunities, are utilising existing networks to help increase distribution efficiency.

❖ *You are now in a position to gain financial freedom by simply joining the most profound business change that has occurred in both America and Britain. Millions of people - and this could include YOU - are involving themselves in the aim for that ultimate goal - <u>financial freedom!</u>*

Chapter Three
The great corporate let-down

Almost 90% of the working population in the United States works for a corporation of some kind - and the figure will not be so very different for Britain. Bankers, artisans, sales people, middle managers and top executives report to these institutions. Even many doctors and lawyers have corporate employers of one sort or another. The corporate employer is the traditional business entity that *rules* our lives.

And *rules* is the operative word!

❖ *While corporate bodies do create jobs and provide income for hundreds of thousands of people, their appeal has begun to diminish. The corporate world is asleep when it comes to rewarding its participants with the real potential of economic freedom.*

The alarm has been sounded. The corporate world has serious shortcomings that can make it impossible for the individual to reach his or her financial goals and dreams.

There are five major failures within the corporate world:

1. The corporate hierarchy.
2. Internal competition.
3. Killing incentives.
4. Resisting change.
5. Denying ownership

Let's look at these in turn...

1. THE CORPORATE HIERARCHY

Who *is* this corporate hierarchy?   It is composed of top managers and executives, immune from the consequences of any bad decisions they may make on a day-to-day basis. They are the people often prone to the common corporate syndrome of *having been promoted to their level of incompetence.* They are the people with the *'let them eat cake'* attitudes towards those who actually do the hard work in the organisation.

In Britain the average salary for the Chief Executive Officer (COE) of a large company is in the region of £180,000.   But who decides the salary levels and fringe benefits of this privileged breed - especially the Chairman of the Board?   In most companies it is the *Board of Directors.* And who is instrumental in appointing the Board of Directors? You've guessed it - *the Chairman of the Board.*

❖ *How does this corporate hierarchy control their corporate world? By controlling information. By setting rules, holding power and utilising the power of fear.*

2. INTERNAL COMPETITION

There is a story about two hikers that exemplifies the attitude to be found in the corporate world.

Bill and Joe were tramping through deep woods when suddenly, on the path ahead, a huge bear reared up , clawing at the air and growling fiercely.   The bear dropped to all fours and started running down the path, directly towards the two men.

Joe thought quickly and took action.   He reached into his back pack and pulled out a pair of running shoes, quickly sat down on the ground, took off his hiking boots, and put on the shoes.

Bill, watched in amazement. *'Joe, what are you doing? You can never outrun a bear!'*

'I don't have to outrun the bear,' Joe panted, *'I only have to outrun YOU!'*

That is the attitude of most career-minded corporate employees: *you don't have to be the best to succeed - you only have to be better than the people you work with.*

Wouldn't it be great if our success depended on the success of others? What if a system existed within which, instead of trying to achieve personal success, everyone helped everyone else to succeed? Even better - if, within that system, people were rewarded because they made others successful?

3. KILLING INCENTIVES

The corporate world is killing incentives. Where is the motivation to succeed? The individual has everything stacked against him.

What is it that motivates people within their job? What gives them the incentive to work? Most of us work out of necessity - and some people really love their jobs. But, if you were not paid, *would you continue to work?*

❖ *Many companies do operate systems of recognition. But, is it enough to be nominated 'Employee of the Month' if, at the end of the month, you haven't enough money to pay the bills?*

Consider this - *you are actually paid the least amount of money it would take to replace you.*

If they could find someone to do the job as well as you do it, but at a lower rate of pay, many companies would jump at the chance to make the change.

❖ *Consider this appalling fact - in the corporate world, you cannot make any more than your boss makes!*
If he or she is underpaid - so are you!

Take the case of Janet - and this is a true story. She was a salesperson for a health care facility. Her job was to sell the concept of health care services to corporations. Her company had never employed anyone in this capacity before but recognised the need, through increased competition, to go out to meet customers. Janet got the job as she had a successful track record with another company. She was paid a basic salary plus commission on sales.

Janet did a superb job and started making sale after sale. Through the commissions she was earning she - and the facility that employed her - began to earn a great deal of money, more even than her bosses who had no share in the increased profits. They did not receive bonus payments when the facility made more money.

So what did the corporation do? *They reduced Janet's rate of commission.*

And what was the corporate reasoning? *We didn't realise you would make so many sales.'*

Janet, you see, had committed the greatest sin in the corporate world - *she had made more money than her boss.*

That, within this antiquated system, cannot be tolerated.

4. RESISTING CHANGE

Resistance to change is not a phenomenon that is strictly limited to the corporate world. Most people dislike and resist change, and yet the future will force you into it, and your survival will depend on it.

The corporate world is still living in the 1950's. At that time, as a general rule, families were together. The man went to work and the woman stayed home with the children. Most people were able to live on one income and still achieve their financial dreams.

❖ *Of course, times have changed, yet the corporate world still sells the myth that if you work and are loyal to the company, you will be successful.*

Try convincing the family with both parents in the corporate work force, day care responsibilities, a large mortgage and a mountain of debts that they have reached their financial dreams. It just isn't so.

Despite the obvious changes in the needs of employees, the corporate world has slept through the uproar.

The typical employee in both America and Britain is a member of a two-worker family - or else a single parent. Corporate policies and practices pretend that this is not so, or simply ignore the statistical facts.

In the United States today, 60% of mothers with young children are full-time employees. Yet most companies do not give them time off when their children are sick. Employees must resign themselves to their children being in day care centres, away from the family - and without achieving their financial goals. Times have certainly changed, but the corporations have not.

5. DENYING OWNERSHIP

❖ *The American billionaire industrialist once gave the following advice on how to be rich - 'the first condition for financial success is to own your own business'*

What does ownership achieve?   Ownership puts you in charge, making you master of your own destiny.   Hard work is directly related to and rewarded with profit.

You make the decisions - you reap the rewards.

To be really successful, risk is necessary.   The trick clearly is to minimise the risk whilst maximising the potential for making money.

Personal business ownership is a remarkable motivational stimulus.   Consider the immigrant families that operate their own businesses.   In the United States, it has been said that immigrants have a four times greater chance of becoming millionaires than do people born in that country.   In Britain the situation is very similar - not many millionaires have emerged yet, but a tremendous commitment to hard work and long hours, often puts the immigrant business man well ahead of his native counterpart.   In both countries, part of the reason may be that so many of them own their own businesses - earning what they are *worth* rather than settling for selling their time for *a set wage.*

Corporations have failed to provide ownership for their employees, and this leads to a terrible situation.   Workers simply *put in time* at work.   They are well aware that extra effort or better performance will not result in long-term economic fitness.   All they have to do is keep out of trouble and hope that redundancy will not be their fate.

Regardless of effort, the rewards will not alter.

A FINAL WORD

The corporate world exists, and the odds are that you work within it.   You don't really need anyone to tell you that it will not meet your financial needs for a better future.   Indeed, it is unlikely that it is meeting your financial needs for the present.

Over the years, a bureaucratic system of doing business has evolved.   The time has arrived when the option is simply *change* or *fail*.   The lure of the corporate myth is strong and almost overpowering.   We, as individuals, are told that we can achieve what, in the United States, is known as *The American Dream* - own a home, take holidays, send our children to good schools, and so on.

But this simply has not proved to be the case.

The myth is exploded.   If you depend on the corporate world for personal financial success,   you are in for a big disappointment.

And Governments are no better!   They are not in the business of rewarding effort and initiative.   In the United States, in the 1930's President Franklin Roosevelt initiated a progressive tax system - a rising tax scale related to the size of your income.   The theory of the day was that every American would soon have a four bedroom house, a car, and all the other trappings of a good lifestyle.   But the fear, pointed out by the economists, was that, once everyone had achieved this dream status, they would all stop work.   So the progressive tax system was instituted to ensure that people never fully achieved their dreams - *and would continue to work.*

41

The highest tax bracket in the United States became 90% - but we, in Britain did even better than that! In the 1970's when we achieved a massive 98% total top rate of tax. This was the time when a rich man had to effectively pay £1 for a 2 pence box of matches!

In the USA, when Ronald Reagan took office, the highest rate was 70% and was greatly reduced during subsequent administrations. But now, in that same country, the rate is slowly climbing back up - some would say, not so slowly. In Britain we now have a top rate of income tax of 40%, but, as we are very aware, indirect taxation imposes its subtle burden in all manner of other ways.

LOOK AT EDUCATION...

We in Britain are always being confronted by statistics about the illiteracy rate in this country, about the number of boys and girls that leave school scarcely able to read and write, and lacking in simple numeracy skills. It is much the same in the United States where TV programmes delight in finding some high school class that couldn't find the United States on a map of the world. The USA is falling behind other industrialised nations in academic standards related to mathematics and the sciences. But, these are not the *real* problems with the educational systems.

❖ *We are teaching our children to function within a system that will no longer meet their needs in the future!*

What do our children understand, for example, about the economics of retirement? These facts were published in *Fortune* magazine in January 1993 as part of a study:

42

THE ULTIMATE GOAL!

*'If a 38 year old couple earned $85,000 per annum in 1993
and intend to retire at the age of 60,   maintaining their
lifestyle, they will need <u>a retirement fund of $4.6 million</u>!'*

Where in our educational systems
do we teach our children facts like this?

Bill Quain, author of the original book of which this is a British adaptation, said he simply did not believe the above facts when first he was confronted with them.   Then his thought was *'why didn't someone tell me this?'* - and he surprised himself with his own honest answer.   *'I am a professor in a College of Business Administration.   If I wasn't telling people this, who would?'*

We are educating our children to become mere cogs in a wheel,   rather than leaders and thinkers.   We are not providing them with the information that they need to make intelligent decisions about their futures.

WHO ARE THE TEACHERS?

We are taught by our parents, by teachers in both schools and universities, and by our peers - not to mention television.
And what are they teaching us?
Both parents and teachers present us with a simple message:
*Study in school, work hard, pay your taxes
and obey the law.*
And the message is, if we do those things, we will be successful, and, to an American, that means achieving *The American Dream.* Our peers taught us to stay in the group, be a team player.   But the problem was, the team wasn't going anywhere either.   If we started to stray from the team to do things the team wasn't doing, they slowly reeled us in.

Our teachers could not teach us to look outside the system, because they were all part of the system. Think about it - what did you learn at school? You learned to add, to write sentences and memorise formulas.

Did anyone ever ask you to *challenge* the system?

Copernicus challenged the system. He discovered that the earth and other planets rotate around the sun.

Columbus challenged the system. He discovered a new world.

Steve Jobs challenged the system. Working in his garage he put unlimited creativity and communication abilities in the hands of millions of ordinary people by developing *Apple* computers.

Rich De Vos and Jay Van Andel challenged the system. They developed a marketing system that enabled millions of hard working people to attain financial freedom through Network Marketing - a multi-level marketing profit sharing structure.

In fact, it is only when we look outside the currently accepted methods of thinking that we make great strides and discover the potential within ourselves.

But we don't let successful people teach us.

Many people are content to sit in front of the television, watching other people lead their lives. We need to find successful people, learn from them and become successful ourselves.

> *Your life is too valuable to trust to someone*
> *who has not succeeded in their own.*

Chapter Four
Let's get personal!

For the sake of British readers, let's take a look at this thing we have always known of as *The American Dream*. As you know, the American title of this book is *Reclaiming the American Dream*. But what exactly *is* it, *and where did it go wrong?*

THE AMERICAN DREAM

Bill Quain is a consultant to *The Knowledge Company,* based in Washington D.C. The company is owned by a lawyer who assists people wishing to emigrate to the United States. He works strictly with professionals, people who have the equivalent of an American college degree. In many cases these professionals will make less in the United States than they did in their home countries.

Bill Quain asked the lawyer why people would go to so much trouble and expense to get a job for less money - the answer was surprising.

❖ *The answer was that people come to the USA for the opportunity - not the money. 'We have the opportunity in the U.S. to create our own freedom...'*

This probably applies in exactly the same way to people in Britain. Isn't it amazing that *we* so readily take this opportunity for granted, whilst outsiders perceive it as the *promise of freedom?* So, this *dream* is based on opportunity. It is the starting point for plotting our individual route to financial freedom.

TRADING TIME FOR MONEY

The point at which, in America, they began to lose *The American Dream,* was when they started *trading time for money.* This happens in exactly the same way in Britain when the individual gives up the idea of business ownership and takes a job. Trading time for money produces several problems:

1. You only have a limited amount of time, therefore, the amount of money you can earn is limited too.
2. Instead of being your own boss, you give someone else power over your future.
3. Due to global competition and the ever-present threat of *'corporate restructuring'*, there is no longer any real job security.
4. When you stop trading time for money, you stop getting money.

Indeed, if you trade your time for money, you are helping someone else achieve their dreams. Your dreams, hopes and aspirations are not important. But, to state the point again, the most appalling part of trading time for money is the simple fact that when you stop, so does the money.

❖ *Yet, there is absolutely no reason why you should actually have to work for the rest of your life. If you receive residual income, your income continues even if you are not actually putting in time. This is freedom!*

Residual income is created ownership. If you own your company, you receive income long after you stop working.

Now, at this point in our exploration, consider the following definition of *The American Dream...*

❖ *Use the opportunities you have to build your own business, create residual income, and set yourself financially free. Make the choices you think are best for you and your family.*

...wouldn't you agree that this has got to be better than trading time for money?

RETIREMENT - HOW?

Have you ever heard anyone say *'I can't wait to retire and live on Social Security'*? Of course not! Most people would hope that they would benefit from an occupational pension - *as well as* any State benefits for which they may qualify. Surveys in the United States have revealed that the majority of people are living in cloud cuckoo land so far as retirement income is concerned. The concept of being able to tuck away a sufficient regular amount from a taxed occupational income, to eventually provide a realistic retirement income, is simply beyond most people's hopes and, indeed, abilities.

In Britain, as far back as the early 1980's the Adam Smith Institute made a report to the government pointing out that the state pension scheme was doomed to failure and bound to collapse eventually. This was based on two simple facts:

1. The number of employed people is constantly reducing as technology takes over more and more of the work, and...

2. Due to advances in medical science, people are living longer.

47

The potent combination of an increasing elderly population being supported by a reducing working population just cannot be expected to work indefinitely, leaving many people stuck with this unacceptable situation.

There is sufficient statistical evidence in the United States - and surely the figures would not be very different here - to support.....

THE 40/50 PLAN

❖ *Under this plan, you can expect to:*
   1. *Work 40 to 50 hours per week.*
   2. *Work 50 weeks per year.*
   3. *Work for 40 to 50 years.*
   4. *End up living on 40 to 50%*
      of what you can't live on now!

Is there a familiar ring to this?   *There should be!*
The majority of people employed in the workforce today are on this plan.   Of course, you might be an exception - *you might work more than 40 to 50 hours a week.*

A survey published in Britain in October 1995 stated that two thirds of the nation's workforce put in anything over 50 hours per week - some as much as 60 hours.   The driving force behind these statistics was said to be the ever-present threat of the dole queue.

The 40/50 plan is our price for stability and dependability. The problem is that when we place our fates in the hands of others,   they will place too low a price on our security.   The free men and women among us,   the entrepreneurs and adventurers, will reap the rewards of freedom.

But what happens when we lose our freedom of choice?
For many people that question isn't answered until they retire. Then they find themselves in the uncomfortable position of being financially dependent on family or government.

In 1989 the U.S. Department of Health, Education and Welfare produced some sobering statistics on people just starting their careers. By the time they reach the age of 65...

- 29% will be dead.
- 13% will have incomes under $5,200.
- 55% will have incomes less than $33,000, with an average income of only $7,300.
- *Only 3% will have incomes over $33,000.*

These are the sort of facts that severely limit your choices!

PLANNING FOR THE FUTURE
Some sobering predictions about retirement in the U.S.A...

- 95% of all Americans reaching the age of 65 will not be able to afford the luxury of financial independence.
- 22% will have to go on working.
- 38% will have to rely on public charity of one sort or another.
- 45% will have to depend on their relatives.
- Only 5% will have sufficient money to meet their financial needs.

❖ *Only 1% of retired people will enjoy the financial independence and <u>dignity</u> that retirement should hold.*

What kind of life is that? Where is the quality of life in that? Imagine working 40 to 50 years and, at the end, having nothing to show for it - *but this is not a 'what if' situation.* This is reality, it is what is happening right now and, unless you do something about it, *it will happen to you!*

THE NEW REALITIES

In an article entitled *'How to protect your financial future' (Fortune* magazine,   1/93), the author discusses realities which we will not have to wait until retirement to experience.

1.   Salaries and wages that no longer keep up with inflation, causing living standards to decrease and making saving for the future nearly impossible.
2. The fact that most middle class families depend on two incomes, and about 63% of married women work.
3. For most Americans, retirement is a fading dream. Today, retired people receive about four dollars back from the state for every dollar they put in. However, when today's workers retire the figure will about one dollar for every dollar contributed.
4. Homeowners can no longer depend on the appreciation in value of their homes.

It is a stark fact of life in Britain that, following the years of increasing property prices,   many people in this country are suffering the phenomenon known as *negative equity* - the result of paying inflated prices, then being stuck with a property that is no longer worth what was paid for it, and with repayments on high mortgage borrowing. No longer does the expression *as safe as houses* mean anything. They are faced with the nightmare scenario of these commitments, coupled with the ever-present spectre of possible redundancy.

A LOST GENERATION

There are many other signs that *The American Dream* is in peril. Chief amongst these is the plight of *Generation X* - the current twenty-something group.

❖ *For the first time in American history, the current younger generation will have a lower standard of living than their parents.*

According to *Business Week* (19/8/91), these young people are the victims of global competition and declining productivity - a generation that has seen average salaries fall by nearly 19.8% per family. This has happened despite the fact that the majority of families now have two incomes. The result has seriously affected opportunities - and hence *The Dream* - for this group. In Britain, young people have suffered in much the same way. Ability counts for remarkably little if opportunity is absent, and, when that is the case, demotivation and diminishing self-esteem are the almost inevitably outcome. In America...

- Home ownership has not only been postponed, it has dropped dramatically.
- Many young adults are forced to live with their parents.

- Unemployment is high. Those who do work are more likely to have part-time jobs.
- Their children are more likely to live below the poverty line.
- It is the first generation to live without the hope of achieving the lifestyle of their parents.

But the woes that have engulfed *Generation X* are not just limited to the twenty-somethings. Many parents had not bargained for their adult children living with them. This unexpected, and possibly, unwished-for fact of life has seriously affected the lifestyle, and limited the choices, of the older generation.

❖ *We are in a crisis!*
Let's face the facts together and do something about it!
Don't pretend that the economic future
of each of us is not in peril.

In short, there is a constant struggle just to maintain the status quo - and that is not a satisfactory situation in itself. We can continue the struggle on the basis of gaining a little, losing some. Or we can make the decision to take advantage of the unique opportunities this situation could offer.

DREAMS, DREAMS!
Peter's family and friends thought he had one fault - Peter was a dreamer. He wanted certain things in life. When he and Jeannine decided to get married, Jeannine's parents were worried that this dreamer would never be able to take care of their daughter.

It has turned out that Peter's ability to dream has been his greatest asset, for at 23, he and Jeannine have created their own part-time business. They have made a significant contribution to their income, and are creating the sort of lifestyle their friends may never achieve. Why?

Because they had a dream and acted on it.

Peter and Jeannine translated their dream into realistic and obtainable goals. They then developed a plan to reach these goals. They were determined that *nothing* was going to deflect them from those goals.

What happens to our dreams?

For most people, they are simply lost in the mad rush to keep up with the financial demands of reality.

What is reality for most people?

It is a mortgage, keeping up the car payments, paying off the credit cards, educating, clothing and feeding the children. Even for a two-worker family, it is hard to have dreams when you are constantly short of the money and time necessary to simply maintain the lifestyle you have.

Dreams are available, free of charge, to all of us. Don't devalue your dreams by minimising them. Go for it! If you don't, at this moment, have a dream, be brave enough to seek one. Nobody else can help you with this - it is a very personal search through the rag bag of hopes and aspirations we all carry with us on our journey through life.

Are you brave enough? *Or are you going to allow others to dictate the limits of your hopes?*

This book cannot give you a dream -
but what it can do...
is to show you a vehicle for reaching your dreams.

SETTING GOALS

Before anything can happen, you must meet two conditions.

❖ *First you must believe that there is some way*
for ordinary people to achieve their dreams.
Secondly, you must firmly establish specific goals.

In this book, we will outline a way for ordinary people to reach their dreams. But that is not the precise purpose of the book. *HOW* you will reach your goals is not the important issue - *WHY* you are trying to reach them *is the supremely important issue.*

So let's talk about the *WHY.*

You should set goals because you deserve more from life than you have right now. Settle for little, and that is what you will get. Never settle for anything simply because that is the way things are today. The question to pose is *do you know what you want?* What is important to you? What would be the single most significant aspect of your life that you would be willing to fight to improve?

At the end of the book there is a short *Appendix* designed to help you decide what your priorities are - is most important to you. Why not look at this right now, and make a few decisions before you read on?

Most people, when asked what is most important to them, list the following...

▪ Family	▪ Religion
▪ Health	▪ Travel
▪ Recreation	▪ Security

54

These are all noble aspirations - and are all things that money cannot buy. However, *money can certainly make a difference!* If leisure and recreation are important to you, then you need two things - *time and money.* Money can buy you time. Money - and the time to enjoy it - means freedom.

Money is not a guarantee of health, but stress is a major source of illness and heart attacks. And lack of money can cause major stress.

Financial security is not a condition for having a family, but the major cause of marital discord is arguments over money.

Perhaps you would like to help some favourite charity or be able to aid families less fortunate than yours? Increasing your financial resources could certainly make a difference!

THE COURAGE TO CHANGE

By now you should realise that your lifestyle is in danger. There is little doubt about that. But what will you do about it? Will you ignore it and hope it improves, or will you face the future with courage and conviction, faith and commitment? One thing you must realise is that *if you want your situation to change, it is you that must change first.* Your thinking must change and you must allow yourself the indulgence of deep desire - desire for, and belief in the possibility of change, and desire for the achievement of all your goals.

There will be many times in your life when the facts will rise up to challenge your basic beliefs. After all you have been brought up by both parents and teachers to believe that hard work is the road to achievement - in the case of American children, to reach out for *The American Dream.*

Well, right now, the facts are probably challenging your beliefs. And, it is time to accept the facts and make some basic changes in your life.

This takes courage. The courage to change and the courage to start all over again. This is not to suggest you should abandon your job! You are going to need the security of a regular pay cheque while you are building the foundations for your financial freedom. But you must prepare for change, to set goals, and to work with people who have already been successful.

GET HELP FROM THE EXPERTS

If you needed an operation, you wouldn't ask a neighbour or a relative to operate on you. In exactly the same way, if you need to make changes to your financial life, you would not seek the advice and opinion of people who have not tasted success. It is far easier to fail than it is to succeed, and the world is full of good-hearted advisors who have never tasted success themselves.

It takes real courage to associate with successful people, not to mention ambition and enthusiasm. Seek out successful people, and emulate them.

❖ *If you follow their example, you will have what they have. If you continue doing what you are doing now, why should you expect to have a different lifestyle five years from now?*

Take courage from the wisdom of successful people. They are no different from you. They were simply fortunate enough to find a business system that could routinely produce successful results. They were willing to pay the price and not allow anything to stop them from realising their dreams.

Chapter Five
The plight of the professional

Being a professional of any sort is not the bed of roses many people believe. Their situation is often fraught with stress. In the United States a doctor can expect to have his first heart attack around the age of 54. The incidence of alcoholism and even suicide amongst doctors in Britain is surprisingly high.

Consider a doctor's training. His or her basic training followed by hospital internment can take up literally years of a young life, and he or she is often well into their thirties before they are earning a good salary. During that period they work hours that no union would permit, or even consider remotely reasonable. They are subjected to the whims and arrogant personalities of teaching consultants, and the excessive hours of duty hospitals impose on the young houseman. The dedication that motivated them into wanting to enter the medical profession must be stretched to the limits by the regime through which the medical student and young doctor are put. And, when they eventually finish their formal training, the likelihood is that they are burdened down with debts related to their educational years. What a wonderful launch to a professional career!

A doctor's earnings may seem good until one recognises the working hours that go with the territory. A former paediatric neurologist in Florida summed up the situation by saying that most doctors create a lifestyle for their families, not for themselves. He tells of the time he returned home from work, late at night, and was almost bitten by the family dog. It seems that the dog did not recognise him!

A doctor may have a good car, a pleasant home, be a member of the golf club and send his children to good fee-paying schools, but he starts his day early, seldom sees his home in daylight and gets 'bleeped' away from the table when dining out, or has his sleep disturbed - sometimes by thoughtless people whose problems could wait until the next day. He is a professional - yet he works hours that no artisan would even consider.

Being in medical partnership is not much better. Although many of the burdens are shared, that can also mean that if one partner is ill, his patients must be looked after by the others in the practice, adding even more to their responsibilities.

In Britain even more stress is heaped on the G.P. by the beaurocracy of the NHS and the endless mound of paperwork that threatens to engulf him in running his practice.

OTHER PROFESSIONALS

Solicitors, engineers, architects and many other professionals suffer from the same problems, in varying degrees. Each must put in long hours to compete - and this competition often exists both within the firm as well as outside.

The fresh young lawyer is expected to work long hours in order to attract the respect of partners. And when partnership is attained he or she is expected to continue to produce. The pressure is always there, the stress is always there. He may eventually build sufficient equity to be offered a partnership. This could mean the eventual possibility of retirement on a sizeable residual income, but only after years of hard work, always accompanied by the stress factor. This, however, could be better than working for a large company and having no residual income at all upon retirement.

WHAT DO PROFESSIONALS WANT?

For many professionals, especially doctors, more money will not solve the problems in their lives. In his research for the original version of this book, Bill Quain listened to many doctors talking about their disappointments in their professional lives. It is not the type of work they do that upsets them, it is the red tape and the constant pressure. According to *Newsweek* (4/93), 40% of doctors interviewed said that, if they had their lives over again, they would not go into the same profession. Somewhat surprisingly, 40% of medical students claimed that a doctor tried to talk them out of going into the profession!

Lawyers and other professionals involved in partnerships make the same sort of complaints. They are responsible for chargeable hours. Every conversation, every piece of filing becomes something that is chargeable to the client. These people claim they are experiencing losses - time is the asset they value the most, and it is that that they are short of each day.

For a doctor, time is a precious commodity. Look at their waiting rooms. People are dealt with as quickly as possible. But a doctor's practice needs the services of nursing staff, clerical staff and cleaners. Insurance costs must be met, telephone bills paid, heating, lighting - the list is endless. To pay all these monthly bills, the doctor must see more and more patients.

What most doctors need is *more time*. Time to enjoy their families, time to spend money - and time to practice the sort of medicine that most of them entered the profession for in the first place.

But, under the current system, time is their enemy. The beeper can go off at any time, more patients must be seen, the bills must be paid, and the doctor will relentlessly approach the age when it is no longer physically possible to maintain that gruelling schedule.

THE PROFESSIONAL'S SCARCEST RESOURCE

If a solicitor wishes to make more money, he or she can do one of two things. They could work longer hours - fine, except for the fact that there are only so many hours in a day. They could employ more staff, or take on a partner to do some of the work. This will increase the volume of work that can be handled, but it also adds to overheads and puts even more stress and pressure on the solicitor's time as people need to be supervised and clients want to see the solicitor, not his assistants. Time runs out.

There is a third alternative - he could charge more for his time. This is also fine up to a point, but fees can only be raised so far otherwise he may price himself out of the market.

The scarcest resource for most professionals is time. In the case of many professionals, *he* is his greatest asset. If he goes on holiday, not only does the holiday cost him money, but earnings cease while overheads go relentlessly on.

So the only thing the professional can sell or trade for money *is his time*, and as we have seen, *that is a limited resource*. Really he is little better off than the employee of a large company. He has the advantage of being owner or partner in his own business but has to accept all the responsibilities and liabilities that go with the territory.

DUPLICATION: *The secret of success*

People become professionals for a variety of reasons. There is the prestige that goes with the profession, there is money, there may be an enviable lifestyle etc. But what if there was a way for professionals to attain these things without all the stress and uncertainty that they now endure, or at best, accept? Would such a situation be of interest to many professionals...?

The answer is to find a system that can be duplicated. A system where each member of the team has the same ability and incentive to generate income. Where no longer is there one earner and a lot of assistants. A system in which each person can equally share both responsibility and the rewards. And the ideal situation would be one in which the rewards would include time, space, independence, status, wealth and an enjoyable lifestyle.

By duplicating themselves, a new breed of business professionals have put this theory into action. These people have created a system that is easy to use and produces fantastic results when diligent effort is applied. Reward for some people is money. To others it is time. Still others enjoy the prestige and status that business success brings.

There is a saying that goes...
Give a man a fish and he will have one meal.
Teach him to fish and he will feed his family for life.

This is the essence of duplication.

Teach someone a simple system of duplication and income-producing ideas, then stand back and join in the rewards. You receive income, not only from your own work, but from the work of others. And everyone has an equal opportunity, regardless of education, qualifications or previous experience.

John Paul Getty once said: *'I would rather have 1% of the effort of 100 men than 100% of the effort of one man.'*
If a professional cannot duplicate his or her work, and most cannot, they are limited *to the effort of one person.*

SO, WHAT DO THEY DO?

In order to break the cycle, there are three necessary steps anyone can take, whether they are a professional or not.

> **First:** recognise the trap of trading time for money
> in a non-duplicating profession.

> **Second:** find a self-employed business system
> that will make money *and*
> will help create a duplicating work force.

> **Third:** put the same kind of effort into a system
> that they put into attaining the qualifications for
> the profession or occupation they now serve.

This book is about a system.
It may not be the answer to every professional's predicament, but it has worked for hundreds of thousands of people all over the world. Systems require work. But the work then produces both time and money. The time is yours to enjoy. The money is in the form of residual income.

Most people are looking for two simple objectives:
economic relief - and the time to enjoy it.

CHAPTER SIX
Profit Sharing - why it works

What motivates people to work? For most of us it is simply the fact that if we didn't work we would starve. Actually, in both the United States and Britain, that is not exactly true - and this raises some interesting questions about why we work, and how we can work better.

SURVIVAL vs. SELF ESTEEM
Many people, especially if they have attended a management course, will be familiar with Maslow's *hierarchy of needs*.

Maslow determined that we fill our most basic needs first, then look for higher level rewards. For example, we are not really concerned about status until we have made sufficient money to feed our families and provided for other basics such as shelter. Once we have attained the basics, we are interested in things such as respect and self esteem.

Most of us know that, if we lost our job, we would still have enough to eat, courtesy of the state aid or charitable organisations - we can depend on our governments for the most basic needs. We have a safety net.

So, why don't we simply stop working and let the government feed and clothe us? It has to be said, of course, that some people do just that. But *most* of us have both *pride* and *self respect* - and to protect these attributes, we have a need to lead productive lives.

In Britain, as in America, economic recession has been responsible for vast numbers of people being laid-off or made permanently redundant. The greatest initial blow is the immediate loss of earnings.   But the permanent damage is to self esteem,   causing feelings of inadequacy and indignity at the situation - this leading,   in many cases,   to physical or even mental problems.   Psychiatrists have pointed out that redundancy can produce all the same feelings as a close bereavement.

❖ *We work to create a proud , dependable and fulfilling life style - not simply to support our families at subsistence level.*

FREE ENTERPRISE
In a free enterprise system, we are all mini companies.   We should use our talents to create wealth.   If we work for someone else, we are creating wealth for them, but, if we work for ourselves, or if we participate in profit sharing, we create wealth for ourselves.

❖ *The portion we receive should be directly proportional to the contribution we make.*

This is what separates free enterprise and capitalism from communism.   In a communist state everyone receives the same pay and benefits, no matter how hard they work.   This is why communism will never survive.   Why should people work hard when, no matter what they do, they will have the same rewards,   respect and lifestyle as everyone else? The result of this is poor workmanship, shortages of everything, poorly maintained roads and services - in short, no real real quality of life at all.

Unfortunately though,   our free enterprise system has begun to crumble as well.   We are trading our enterprise for security, and that security has a price. We can never make the money we need to steadily improve our lifestyle. A wage slave, no matter how well he is paid, is still a slave.

In a truly free enterprise system we should be able to make as much money as our dreams, ambitions and talents allow. There should be no ceiling on earnings.

PROFIT SHARING

In recent years many companies have instituted what they call profit sharing. Under this system employees are given compensation, usually by way of shares, that enable them to participate in the profits of the company. In theory the shares are awarded in proportion to the value of the employees' contribution. In reality the profit sharing is more likely to be in direct proportion to the employees' earnings - especially where the profit sharing is related to any form of retirement package attracting tax relief.

We in Britain have been made very aware of the unseemly scramble amongst top executives of large companies, especially the recently privatised facilities, such as water, gas and electricity, for higher salaries and profit sharing schemes of fairly startling proportions. The *House of Commons Employment Committee* recently stated in a report on the remuneration of directors: *'We believe that those executives in the privatised utilities who have combined drastic changes to their workforces - including major redundancies - with high increases in remuneration for themselves should have shown greater sensitivity in handling pay and redundancy issues.'*

❖ *If top executives are interested in maximising their profit sharing, we can assume that it is a good idea for all of us to participate in profit sharing!*

The sad truth is that most of us will never have it - certainly not in the manner we deserve.

THE ORIGINAL CONCEPT

Profit sharing was traditionally operated throughout the fishing industry. At the end of each voyage, the captain or owner of a vessel would subtract the expenses of each trip and distribute the remainder amongst the crew. This was very motivational; the crew worked willingly to produce the largest catch possible in the knowledge that they would be proportionally rewarded. There was no union interference, everyone pulled together and was rewarded accordingly.

In most industrial situations these days, the concept of *'as you sow, so shall you reap'* has gone right out of the window. We are paid what the job is worth, *not what we are worth.*

Industry simply does not like employees earning too much. Yet, their fears are groundless. There should be no ceiling on the amount that any employee could make. If the employees are making a lot, that must be the greatest indicator of a highly successful business. But the reality is not like that - *an employer will pay you the least amount that it would take to replace you.* There is always someone willing to take your place. They may not do the job as well as you, but if there are wage and salary ceilings, nobody will do their job as well as they really could if there were more incentives. After all, the company will always make higher profits if it can employ someone to do the job for less.

❖ *If companies simply linked pay to performance, you would earn more - and so would they*

EMPLOYEE OWNERSHIP

So, profit sharing is great! The only problem is, when profits cease, there is no longer anything to share. Employee ownership is a long-term, highly motivational practice that can make a huge difference to retirement income.

❖ *If you OWN part of a company you continue to reap the benefits of profits, even after you stop working. If you are sick or disabled, the work that you have already done will continue to contribute to your financial security.*

Of course, ownership has a price. It may be necessary to sacrifice some of the immediate rewards to create equity for the future. For most of us, that would be fine, if we end up with residual income that continues to produce regular payments even after we have stopped producing for the company.

A number of companies have developed employee ownership plans, and their progress has been watched with interest. Unfortunately, in the majority of cases, they only *appear* to provide real ownership. Dr. Donald Schon, a professor at the well-known Massachusetts Institute of Technology, observed that only 5% of all the companies listed as having employee ownership in the book *'The New Owners'*, actually practised a realistic form of this motivational system. In addition, a mere one half of one percent of the companies were truly owned and operated by the employees.

Will *you* enjoy residual income when you stop working?
Will you be able to stop working when you like?
Or will you work the *40/50 plan* and live on state benefit.
The choice is yours...

...but it is a choice you must make now!

THE NEW BREED

So, here are the facts:

Your company may have profit sharing, but it will not produce residual income. Your company may operate a share option scheme, but this will not give you a chance to directly influence the company's performance or direction.

You may even own your own business but you are limited by the amount of time you can put into it.

The economy is in trouble with little sign of immediate recovery - and you want security for your family.

What do you do?

❖ *Rather than burden yourself with all the worries of running your own business - employees, overheads, premises, equipment, administration - why not investigate the possibilities offered by Network Marketing?*

After 20 years of business ownership, business education and teaching, and after 2 years of careful analysis in this particular field, Bill Quain, the author of *'Reclaiming the American Dream'*, earnestly makes the recommendation that, a few years ago, might have caused him second thoughts...

❖ *You should investigate the possibilities offered in Network Marketing.*

The reason such a statement cannot be considered bold any longer is that Network Marketing companies, since the mid 1980's, have entrenched themselves with significant market shares and have continued to greatly out-perform their traditional competitors.

This has not happened to quite the same extent in Britain, since the Network Marketing leaders all had their roots in the United States and only found their way to this country relatively recently. We have not *grown up* with the situation in quite the same way as the Americans, but, nevertheless, many of the big names in Network Marketing now flourish and grow within our shores, often using Britain as a jumping off platform to spread eventually into Europe.

The system, also known as Multi-level Marketing (MLM), can provide an income stream that continues to grow even as direct involvement decreases. Network Marketing takes advantage of the power of duplication to make money and create a good lifestyle. We will discuss the details of Network Marketing in the next few chapters - for now, let's concentrate on the reasons people like you are increasingly moving towards this opportunity.

Both the United States and Britain have a Direct Selling Association (DSA), and in both countries most successful Network Marketing companies are members. In America, Amway, Mary Kay Cosmetics, Nu Skin etc. are members of the DSA, and that organisation conducted a survey to determine why people became involved with these companies. The survey asked its respondents to rank their reasons for creating a business of their own.

Consider these results:

■ 87.5% said liking for and belief in the products
was very important.
■ 61% rated supplemental income as very
important.
■ 51% were very attracted by the concept of pay
related to effort.

Also, according to the DSA survey, participants saw the
following *opportunities* in the business:

■ Personal and professional growth.
■ Being your own boss.
■ Anyone can be successful.
■ Flexible working hours.

The new breed of entrepreneur has limited the risk by limiting
the investment and cutting out the overheads. Yet, he or she
can take advantage of the full benefits of duplicating their
efforts.

In a Network Marketing company your work is
duplicated by those in your *down-line*. If you put in eight
hours a week, and have six distributors in your down-line
working eight hours, who each have four people in their
down-line working eight hours, there is a total of 248 hours
of work per week in your organisation.

❖ *You profit from 248 hours of work, yet you have only*
worked eight. That's duplication, and that's power!

Your working hours = 8
plus
6 distributors working 8 hours = 48

plus
24 distributors(6 x 4) working 8 hours = 192

Total = 248 hours of work

This new breed of entrepreneur has discovered an ethical, legal and simple way to make money and buy back their time. Network Marketing (MLM) is a system that has been around for almost 40 years, but is only now beginning to realise its full potential in the USA.   Here in Britain the system is gathering momentum fast as people realise that this opportunity, when treated seriously, has the potential to place wealth in the hands of *anyone* prepared to work for it.

The question is - *are you courageous enough to face facts and make a change in your life?*   If the answer is *yes,* then read the remainder of this book as though your financial life depended on it - *and it probably does!*

CHAPTER SEVEN
Modern marketing - 3 P's and a D

Multi-level or Network Marketing is not a brand new development. It really gained its fame when the Nutralite Vitamin Company (now owned by the Amway Corporation) implemented the concept in the 1950's. Today there are hundreds of companies using the multi-level approach. Some of the biggest names in consumer goods and services use this distributive system.

In the United States, perhaps the most familiar are the long distance telephone companies who employed Network Marketing methods to persuade their customers to sign up their friends and family, thereby qualifying for discounts on their own telephone use. The idea was that those people would do the same, thus building a network. One telephone company joined forces with Amway, the longest standing Network Marketing company, so that Amway distributors could make money by creating a network of users for the telephone company.

❖ *This is the very essence of Network Marketing - creating a network of consumer/merchants who use and market the product and tell others how to do the same, then profit-share, residually and long term, in direct proportion to the volume of business created.*

But to understand Network Marketing it is first necessary to understand the overall marketing concept, so let's now discuss the *evolution* and *revolution* of this modern marketing concept.

MARKETING TRENDS

The principles of marketing are based on one assumption -
anything can happen!

Having a good product is not enough in itself. That product
has to be placed firmly in the hands of the consumer - and
there is no easy way of determining just how the consumer
will react to either a product, or to its advertising. Marketing
is unlike physics or chemistry, where the mixing of certain
ingredients in certain proportions will produce a
predetermined reaction that will happen every time. In
marketing, nothing is predictable, reaction least of all.

Who could have predicted the popularity of ethnic food
take-aways, military styled four-wheel-drive vehicles, the
health food craze, or video games?

There have always been misconceptions about Network
Marketing. For example many people still labour under the
delusion that it is door-to-door selling. Some people have the
mistaken idea that it has some connection with chain letters!

In the 1980's many people took a look at this distributive
concept - then more commonly known as *Pyramid Selling* -
and, for one reason or another, did nothing about it - and
have not taken another look since. Perhaps you were one of
these? If you were, ask yourself whether you would ever
have imagined that...

1. You would walk up to a hole in the wall outside
   your bank and get money out of a machine?
2. That your mother or your spouse would learn how
   to use self-service petrol pumps at a garage?
3. That you and your spouse would both have to
   work full time just to afford a three bedroom house?

Modern marketing has responded to new technologies and consumer demands.

❖ *Network Marketing is not a new idea, but it has changed to meet the needs of our times. It will continue to grow and change because it is based on people skills, not product skills.*

THE MARKETING VARIABLES

There are two types of marketing variables - controllable and uncontrollable. It is the marketing expert's job to identify the uncontrollable variables and to create a product and a promotional plan to work within those defined limits. He must also be aware of the need to adjust the controllable variables to make them fit into the world's realities.

At first sight that might sound a little confusing. Let's explore the types of marketing variables, and see how they fit the Network Marketing mould.

CONTROLLABLE VARIABLES

Until recently controllable variables were called *The four P's of Marketing.* They were...

Product...Price...Promotion...Place

Products are goods or services. Price is the amount charged for the product. Promotion is the mixture of advertising and personal selling, and place is the retail store at which the products are sold - often known as *the point of sale.*

Today the overwhelming emphasis has shifted so far from *place* to *distribution*, that many marketing people no longer discuss the marketing *Four P's*. Instead they emphasise the *Three P's and a D.*

77

❖ *Distribution has replaced place! It is no longer necessary to have retail outlets to put the goods and services into the hands of the consumer.*

In the United States, manufacturers such as *Nike* shoes and *Firestone Tyres*, as well as service providers like *Walt Disney* and *Hyatt Hotels* are utilising the power of Network Marketing companies to distribute their products.

❖ *Distribution will be the key to success in the 1990's and beyond*

UNCONTROLLABLE VARIABLES

- Economic
- Technological
- Political/legal
- Sociological
- Competitive

The marketing expert has very little control over variables such as these, yet they have a great influence over the way in which goods and services are sold and distributed. So, controllable variables must be used to respond to the uncontrollable variables. For example, as Paul Zane Pilzer points out in *'Unlimited Wealth'*, Americans in the 1960's ate only 5% of their meals outside their own homes. Today they eat 50% of their meals in restaurants. What created that demand? Changes in the uncontrollable variables created opportunities for marketing people to utilise their controllable variables.

In response to declining living standards (an economic variable), more and more women began to enter the workforce. This created two factors. Firstly there was less time for these women to prepare dinner at home (sociological), and secondly, families had more disposable income (economic). Companies began to create restaurant concepts that were able to serve a limited menu quickly (competitive), and Congress enacted legislation to control franchising (political/legal). Communications equipment, computerised cash registers, and microwave ovens (technological) made the consumers more conscious of speed and efficiency. They begun to expect even faster service.

The restaurateurs used controllable variables to respond to the demand. They created the *fast food* concept (product) that focused on a few, easy to prepare items. They offered less service, but at a lower price (price). They knew that if they could capture the attention of children, they could get the rest of the family too, and create a loyal, lifetime clientele.

So they advertised to the youngsters (promotion). Finally they made the food available in as many locations as possible (place), and even created drive through windows and satellite locations in shopping malls and schools (distribution).

Whilst this is rather simplified, it does demonstrate the use of controllable and uncontrollable variables.

UNCONTROLLABLE VARIABLES AND MLM
Let's look at the way in which uncontrollable variables affect Network Marketing companies.

Economic

Much of this book has been dedicated to exposing the inequities of the economic system that have been created by the corporate world. People are *looking* for answers to their economic conditions. Network Marketing can provide that resource.

In addition, most MLM companies offer profit sharing and ownership to individuals, and the concept connects effort to rewards. The system offers new companies an opportunity to distribute their products without some of the massive start-up costs, and this enables more products to reach the marketplace.

The founder of the Nu Skin company was able to build his organisation's sales to $500 million in 1991 without a paid national sales force. This, it is said, allowed him to spend more money on product development and profit sharing.

Technological

Technological changes have created vast opportunities for wealth generation through MLM. An entrepreneur can start his or her business with just a telephone. Then, with a home office, a computer, modem and fax machine, huge networks can be managed efficiently. Of course, there will never be a total substitute for face-to-face contact - but who would have predicted the huge boom in computer, television and catalogue sales? We are told the most amazing innovations are yet to come.

Political/legal

In the USA, Network Marketing companies are controlled and regulated on both a national and state level, indeed, they are often held to a higher standard than other companies.

In Britain, there is legislation controlling all aspects of MLM operation and, at the moment of writing, there is a consultative document from the DTI moving through the industry exploring any need for further controls. Any changes in the legislation will be eventually based on the outcome of this document.

Unfortunately, there are unscrupulous members to be found in any profession or industry, and MLM has had its share. But then so has the property market, medicine, the law and politics. When the American stock market scandals of the 1980's occurred, people did not stop investing their money on Wall Street. When the Rackman property scandals were exposed in London, people did not stop renting property. There have been a few unfortunate incidents in Network Marketing on both sides of the Atlantic, and these have, paradoxically, been instrumental in tightening up the legislation. But the fact that the big names still thrive and grow proves that basically the system is very sound indeed. Just as most barrels contain the odd bad apple, reputable companies will never be injured by the odd bad operator - the sort of people who could equally well show up in any industry.

According to *New Business Opportunities* magazine (10/92), the Federal Trade Commission charged that the Amway company, *'one of MLM's biggest and most respected companies'* was an illegal pyramid. On May 8th 1978 they were cleared after four years of legal battle.

'If Amway hadn't withstood the FTC's challenge, there would be no MLM industry today' said Jeff Babener of Babener Associates, and Oregon based firm specialising in direct merchandising issues.

In America MLM companies are regulated by the FTC under Article five which prohibits unfair trade practices. Companies that make exaggerated claims or operate as an illegal pyramid, can be prosecuted. This regulation has helped to insure that reputable MLM companies will not be injured by the few bad operators who seem to show up in every industry.

In Britain the Network Marketing industry operates under two Parliamentary *'Statutory Instruments'*, safeguards for both the MLM companies and their distributors. The Department of Trade and Industry (DTI) have produced an excellent pamphlet explaining the legislation for the layman.

Of course, legal and political activity also affects potential distributors. Many doctors and dentists, for example, have chosen Network Marketing to provide stability against uncertain times, the stress of the job and the ever-present uncertainty of possible changes in health care legislation that could affect their professional careers.

Sociological

The economical changes that have driven 63% of married women in the United States into the work force have created sweeping sociological changes. In a more mobile society families are as likely to move to fit the woman's career as that of the man. The traditional extended family is certainly less visible, and grandparents are often no longer on hand to help raising the family. A further aspect of sociological change is that people have less time to shop.

Enter Network Marketing! *Forbes* magazine (5/93), provides ample information about changing sociological trends and their affect on business. According to *Forbes*, Americans are spending less time in the shopping mall and visiting fewer stores per trip. In addition they are ordering almost twice as many goods and services from catalogues.

In Britain there is a veritable slump in High Street shopping as more and more small businesses go to the wall. At the same time though, the direct mail business flourishes. According to the Direct Mail Information Service, direct mail volume has increased by 116% over the past ten years, whilst direct mail expenditure has shown an increase of 224% over the same period. The average consumer spends approximately £80 per direct mail response and makes an average of 2.47 responses per year.

Changing sociological trends present many opportunities. Single women have learned to be capable managers of both home and the workplace. They have learned to utilise their time better and to have higher aspirations than a generation ago, and they are entering the Network Marketing field and achieving considerable success.

Competition

Competition has two sides to it. The number of firms becoming involved in the Network Marketing business is growing - yet markets for consumer/merchant distributors are far from saturated. The consumer/merchant distributors tend to be very loyal to their products.

❖ *There is a recognisable switch in loyalty from stores to specific brands - a trend that favours the distributor with a reliable product.*

The other competitive factor inherent in Network Marketing is that people work together as teams. Success is built on the success of others, and this powerful concept reduces competition between individuals and encourages people to work together in a network. The new phase of competition was predicted in John Naisbitt's powerful book *'Megatrends'*.

CONTROLLABLE TRENDS AND MLM

Network Marketing is a serious form of marketing and the distributor is on the front line of the marketing company. Let's now briefly consider the implementing of Network Marketing on four controllable variables - and we will return to this topic in more detail later in the book.

Product

The basis of any Network Marketing operation is to have a truly superlative product. It should be guaranteed and backed with the full weight of the company.

Companies such as Amway are very strongly entrenched in Britain and carry their own products as well as lines of other firms. In the case of Amway, over 450 of the *Fortune 500* companies in America distribute their products through the Amway network.

Other Network Marketing ventures move their own products exclusively. Nu Skin is a prime example - also strongly building a British network.

Price

Prices must be competitive, otherwise buyers will simple shop elsewhere. In traditional retailing, low prices often imply less service. In Network Marketing this can never be the case. Whilst Network Marketing companies need to be competitive, because of the very personal involvement, service is usually beyond the customer's expectations.

Network Marketing is far removed from the concept of the wholesale buying club with its aim to create a savings plan. Shopping at discount houses, too, has little power compared to the income stream that Network Marketing creates, continuing and increasing with time. There really is no comparison to the system that creates a profit-sharing pool based on consumer/merchandising habits.

In talking of competitive pricing, there is no implication that Network Marketing companies should or do sell their products at heavily discounted prices. Price is a combination of *product quality, service level and convenience.*

Promotion

Advertising - public relations - direct selling...all of these are considered part of the promotion variable.

A good Network Marketing company supports its salesforce with training, high quality promotional literature, samples, and advertising. The best companies provide their consumer/merchants with a 'packaged' system. It will contain support material for both the retailing of the products and for attracting new consumer/merchants.

Distribution

❖*Network Marketing IS distribution. It is the process of putting products and services directly into the hands of the consumers.*

The best Network Marketing companies embody the following features for the support of their consumer/merchants:

- Constantly maintained stock levels
- Fast delivery

- Free collection for returned items
- An easy ordering system
- Money back guarantee

A FINAL WORD

Merchandising is not an exact science, but the great Network Marketing companies have helped to take some of the mystery and uncertainty out of the process. Their systems are worthy of your investigation. Many thousands of people on both sides of the Atlantic have found financial security and freedom by using this fast evolving economic movement.

If *you* are of the entrepreneurial spirit, you will prosper and gain a deeper understanding of the system that, judging by a track record already established, and the growth rate achieved over the past few years, will probably create the largest form of merchandising the world is likely to see.

CHAPTER EIGHT
What the experts say

Close your eyes and imagine the following...
It has just been announced that an electronic shopping mall - an interactive shopping network - is to open, access to which will be through your television set. Once inside the mall, viewers will be able to browse in the individual shops, all of which will carry well-known brand names. Shoppers will have access to this service at any time, day or night, even on public holidays. They will pay for their purchases by credit card or 'switch' and will have the goods delivered to their homes.

Imagine how convenient this will be! No more queues, no screaming children - yours or anyone else's. No braving the elements when the weather is too hot or too cold and wet.

Does this sound like a dream? It shouldn't. Interactive shopping networks are already on-line. The future is here - now!

In the USA, catalogue shopping is a 51 billion dollar industry already, and it is predicted that advancements like the above will greatly increase their channels of distribution.

❖*Where will you be when Network Marketing goes 'network'? Do you have the vision and determination to grab your piece of the future? Or will you still be listening to some of your friends, ignoring the wave of opportunities that will carry hundreds of thousands into unlimited opportunity?*

How can it be put to you more clearly?
Don't miss this opportunity!

CRISIS ON THE HIGH STREET

We are constantly being made aware of the decline in high street shopping. Whilst feeling some sympathy for the shop keeper and small business owner, it does seem that a modicum of the blame for their plight lies with them. There has been a noticeable decline in service, attention and even in attempts to sell us goods! Yes, even that. It is truly amazing that, with the retail trade in such a plight, so little attention is actually paid to the potential customer. It is as though the notion of how to sell has become a forgotten art. A cloud of lethargy has enveloped the high street. Not only have people lost the habit of spending, the retail trade has lost the ability - it would seem, almost the will - to sell. There is an attitude that is almost akin to a death-wish.

There has been a lot of criticism of the shopping mall in Britain - the depressing anonymity and sameness they present - and yet, to leave their glittering unreality and step out into the real life of city streets is to be greeted, all too often, by boarded-up shops.

A new shopping phenominum in Britain is the 'factory' shop. This is a concept which has been imported from the USA. Developments of such establishments are beginning to take root on the outskirts of towns and cities, presenting a peculiar fantasy, Disney-influenced, 'toy town' High Street of specialist shops. The question that springs to mind is, if the buying public have abandoned the individual High Street shop, why should they take to the inconvenience of travelling out of town to this make believe High Street?

Catalogue sales are on the increase, and mail order appears to flourish. And all the time Network Marketing is growing and expanding, involving more and more people who wish to better their lifestyle. Are we witnessing a slow but relentless decline in traditional methods of trading?

Whilst traditional retail outlets are suffering their decline, Network Marketing is benefiting because of its unique blend of products, information, service and convenience - not to mention the friendly human contact that is one of its great strengths.

The Direct Selling Association publishes interesting statistics on the selling of goods *in the home* - these figures do not include double glazing and home improvements. Between 1985 and 1994 retail sales of this sort almost trebled - from £329 million to £948 million. In 1993, MLM accounted for 23% of all direct sales in the home and in 1994 this figure rose to 31%.

So, what is the next step? To create a store that enters your home with information and products, and a convenient delivery system. That is progress - and it is what consumers want.

And now, just consider this...

❖ *The Wall Street Journal estimates that by the end of the decade, over 50% of all goods and services in the United States will be available through Network Marketing companies.*

...and the Wall Street Journal is not given to flights of fancy!

In *Success* magazine, Nicol Wooley Biggart notes that nothing in recent history in the United States has grown at the speed of direct selling organisations such as Amway, Nu Skin and Mary Kay Cosmetics. Coinsider the astonishing growth of the Amway Corporation internationally. In 1959, sales volume was 500 million dollars. By 1989 it had risen to 1.8 billion dollars. In 1992 it jumped to 3 billion, and at the end of the fiscal year 1995, sales volume had more than doubled to a startling 6.2 billion dollars!

❖*It has been stated that total sales from Network Marketing companies exceed $100 billion per year, and there are estimated to be over seven million people actively involved as distributors in Network Marketing around the world.*

These people are only involved for one reason - they want to change their lives by increasing their spendable income.

THE REVOLUTION IN TECHNOLOGY

Would you deny the computer revolution? It has happened. People *have* adapted to technology. And people *have* changed their buying habits.

Wealth is the result of combining technology with physical resources. That is to say, we have the ability to increase our wealth by moving with the times and changing our technology - regardless of our available physical resources. So if your time is limited, use technology to increase your wealth! If you are not as clever as your neighbour, use technology to increase your wealth. If you are not tall, athletic, handsome, educated - simply use the technology of the day to improve your wealth!

❖ *Technology does not refer to computers!*
It is not fancy machinery!
It is something that is available to everyone!

Technology is simply *knowledge*. If you have read this book to this point, you are already in posession of the knowledge you need to make money - to ultimately allow you, providing you have the determination and commitment to do it, to become totally financially free.

In this case, the technology is networking. In the next chapter we will look at the things you need to be successful in Network Marketing - and they are simple...

commitment - energy - enthusiasm

...and these are all you need to put the technology of networking to work for you.

THEY SAW THE LIGHT

Network Marketing was first discovered by ordinary people who wanted to change their lives, make more money and achieve their dreams. And at first, they were alone. Not any more! Some of America's largest distributive companies recognised the power of this concept until, now, there is virtually no product or service that cannot be moved through Network Marketing. The only remaining barriers were for fresh foods, but even this is changing! Network Marketing will, no doubt, eventually dominate the food chain!

IS THERE HOPE FOR THE NEWCOMER?

You may easily be tempted to ask the question *'...is there still room for the newcomer?'* The answer is an emphatic *'of course there is!'* Some people still have the idea that you must be in at the beginning to prosper in a Network Marketing operation, new or established. The fact is that *wherever* you slot into a down-line development, *you are the apex for everything that happens from that point onwards!*

Another common concern to the newcomer is that of market saturation - but more of that in a moment.

The 'little man' is the backbone of Network Marketing just as the foot soldier is the backbone of the army. We cannot all be generals, and many of us would not want to be. It is the single person, the couple or small group that start the network. There are endless stories of the ordinary person, trapped in an ordinary job, finding Network Marketing and seizing their opportunity to reach out for financial freedom.

Within any Network Marketing down-lines you will find doctors, estate agents, sportsmen and women, mechanics and people from every walk of life. Their one common denominator is wealth - and they obtained that wealth by taking the first step. They shared their business with others, helped them to grow and reaped huge rewards.

YOU are the most important part of the Network Marketing system. The big companies need YOU. And it is YOU that will be rewarded.

SATURATION - *NEVER!*

It is the nature of the free enterprise system that people will always want something. To assume that Network Marketing markets will become saturated is to assume that no new products will be introduced. We know that will not happen.

Some people come up with the notion that before long *everyone* will be involved in the business and there will be nobody to sell to and nobody to teach. Ask yourself this - *is everyone you know involved?* Before you discovered the business, how many people did you know who were involved? Saturation, either in terms of distributors or products has never been known to happen yet, and it is most unlikely it will ever happen in the future. There are just too many people in the world! By way of example, the population of the United Kingdom stands at 57.2 million - and there are currently approximately 120,000 people seriously involved in Network Marketing in the UK. Saturation of the market or the possibility of the entire population becoming involved, would take a long, long time!

Some people, of course, will *never* become involved. They will go on trading their time for money hoping that someday they will become wealthy - that is, if they are not made redundant.

Right now, throughout the whole world, there are not sufficient people in Network Marketing to replace the population of New York City!

In Britain, more people are born each year than are involved in Network Marketing. Have we run out of people to eat pizzas and burgers, buy cars and new homes?

❖ *Fear of saturation is a complete red herring!*
It is a common arguement used by the procrastinator.

CHOOSING YOUR MLM COMPANY

Once you have become convinced that Network Marketing is the route to follow to achieve all your dreams and ambitions, it is obviously important to choose the correct company. Not all Network Marketing companies are created equal. The ideal is to select a company with plenty of potential to grow and support you.

Success magazine (1/93) warned that 85% of all MLM ventures fail within the first 18 months. This statement sounds like sheer alarm and despondency, but the fact is that about the same percentage of *all* new businesses are likely to fail within the same time scale! A company's age is not necessarily any guarantee of success. In making one's choice of a Network Marketing company there are certain sensible things to take account of:

1. The age of the company.
   - *Generally, avoid start-ups.*
2. A good track record and steady sales growth.
3. A sound financial package.
   - *Compensation checks, start-up costs, bonuses, commissions etc.*
   Are there minimum purchase levels or monthly sales requirements?
   Are there any penalties for non-performance?
4. Departmentalisation.
   - *Are there separate departments for distributor relations, accounting etc.?*
5. Products.
   - *Is the product consumable, desirable, affordable - ie.sensibly priced, approved etc?*
   Is the product guaranteed?
   What is the company buy-back policy?
6. The system.
   - *Good companies offer brochures, catalogues, advertising, training and support.*
   Join a company with a good system that can provide all the support you need.

GROW AND BE WEALTHY

There is no doubt that the Network Marketing concept is growing fast - everywhere. It can and will provide opportunities for anyone who wishes to participate with a good company. Naturally, some opportunities will be better than others - this is why is it so important that you choose your company carefully.

All journeys, no matter how long, begin with just one step - and that step is commitment. Once you have decided what you want to do *JUST DO IT!*

There really are no excuses large enough to prevent you from taking advantage of this remarkable system. If you met some of the people who have already done it, you would quickly see, there is nothing special about them. The majority of them never owned a business before in their lives. Yet they have made money and changed the course of their lives.

So it is up to you - *do you have the power to do it, do you have the courage?*

Can you do it?...*Yes, without a doubt - of course you can!*

Will you do it? *Only you can make that choice.* But if you choose not to do it, it is possible that *you may miss the greatest opportunity that has ever been presented to you.*

CHAPTER NINE
How money is made

It is through distribution that Network Marketing companies make the huge profits that are shared with the distributors. Think of it, MLM entrepreneurs are called *distributors*. They have created an alternative distribution system.

As we saw earlier in the book, in the United States, the cost of goods today breaks down into 15% manufacturing costs and 85% *distribution costs*. This includes wholesalers, sales commissions and retail costs - and this is exactly the opposite of what it used to be at the turn of the century, when only 15% of costs were related to distribution. The remaining 85% were incurred during manufacture. The only way in which money could be saved was by cutting costs in the manufacturing process, and vast fortunes were made by inventors who were able to simplify manufacturing. Eli Whitney's *cotton gin* (a machine that separates the cotton fibres from the seed boll) is an excellent example in the United States, whilst, even earlier, in Britain, Arkwright invented a spinning frame, more commonly known as *The Spinning Jenny,* which revolutionised the Lancashire cotton industry. The steam engine had an even more far reaching affect. In America the *Bessemer Furnace* improved steel production. Henry Ford introduced the assembly line, which made it affordable for almost everyone to won a car.

❖ *The greatest opportunities today for creating wealth lie in distribution. It is said that the majority of the largest personal fortunes made in the United States during the past*

97

two decades were made by people who discovered better ways of distributing things. (*Success* magazine 5/93)

NEW ALLIANCES

The cost of stock and distribution has created some amazing alliances among business. The Japanese initiated a cost saving system in the 1970's called *'just in time'* purchasing. Although it applied mostly to manufacturing plants, it is the basis for *'just in time'* retailing, which is the backbone of Network Marketing distribution.

Just in time purchasing was first implemented in American car manufacturing. Instead of carrying enough stock for a month or a week, the car manufacturers began to limit stock needs to just a few hours. This cut their costs of storage and the amount of money tied up in stock. Cash flow was improved and the end result was that they were able to cut the cost of their cars to consumers.

However, it became critical that their suppliers should be able to deliver the raw materials to them at a moment's notice. So the suppliers began to build warehouses right next to the car factories, with the two facilities connected by a rail link. Through this system, the suppliers bore the costs of stock, not the car manufacturers.

It was easier for the suppliers to store the materials as they were the specialists in their particular line. This was a great improvement on the earlier system when the manufacturer had to store great quantities of steel, rubber, vinyl etc.

❖ *The efficiency created by 'just in time' purchasing saved money in the distribution system and made money for both the supplier and the manufacturer.*

A further way of cost-savings on conventional distribution involved eliminating sales representatives, whose commissions add greatly to costs. Advances in communications technology has made this possible by allowing direct contact between parties through sophisticated computer systems.

But why should you be concerned with all this? It is simply to demonstrate that the Network Marketing concept represents the world's best system of distribution, with all the advantages and none of the disadvantages - *and you, as a distributor, will share in the profits!*

WHO BENEFITS - AND HOW?

There are four main beneficiaries from Network Marketing distribution:

1. The Manufacturer.
2. The Network Marketing Company.
3. Distributors.
4. Consumers.

The obvious benefit to the manufacturer is greater income, through both savings and increased sales. The manufacturer benefits from reduced costs because the distributors are almost always independent contractors.

In some cases - Nu Skin is a notable example - the manufacturer and the Network Marketing company are the same entity. Nu Skin distributors only move products that are produced by the Nu Skin company. However, Amway entrepreneurs represent, not only the Amway household line, but also a line of over 5000 different products and services from thousands of other manufacturers, many internationally known.

Distributors can make money in two ways in most Network Marketing companies. Firstly they can retail products, buying them at wholesale prices and selling them at retail prices. Secondly, the MLM companies offer a bonus or override on the volume created in a group of sponsorship.

❖ *This means that large amounts of money that would have been swallowed by the distribution process are held by the Network Marketing company. This money is paid to distributors, based on the amount of volume they generate.*

The money is generally awarded on a sliding scale. A distributor with only a small volume of business might receive a 5% bonus, whilst a distributor turning over a large volume of business could benefit from 25% in overrides from the Network Marketing company. And remember, there is literally no limit on the amounts that can be earned!

The final beneficiary is the consumer. The modern consumer is faced with a serious dilemma - how to get quality products, and value for money, without endlessly trailing around the high street and city shopping centres.

In both Britain and the United States, people are no longer shopping for recreation. They are also spending less of their time in shopping. In Britain, a general malaise of lethargy seems to have crept into the high street in recent times. They have lost the habit of selling - mainly because the consumer has lost the habit of buying, the result of the general economic situation.

A FINAL WORD ON DISTRIBUTION

Distributing goods and services through Network Marketing is profitable right now, but is certainly the wave of the future. In order to take advantage of the financial benefits, a would-be distributor must identify a solid company that has a product that people want. The ideal product is consumable or replaceable so that there is always continuity of sales.

So, why not take a long hard look at the opportunities on offer - *and get started?*
You now have the knowledge, and the understanding as to why Network Marketing distribution works.
Make it work for you!

CHAPTER TEN
The final solution - The People's Franchise!

Money is made in networks. That's true! And here is the great news - *you are already in networks!*

Are you a member of a *Lions* club, are you a *Rotarian*, or a member of a football club? Do you have a wide circle of friends? If you see a good film, do you tell your friends about it? *These are all networks.* We belong to networks because we are human and it is a natural state - in fact, that is the way we operate best. We work with others.

Networkers share their experiences. They help one another. They co-operate.

❖ *Does your employer take a real interest in you?*
Does he ask how he may help you to make more money?
Does he ask if he can help you to reach your dreams?
Probably not - but your network might.

A network is a family of people working together to help one another. Networkers do things for each other. They use their collective skills to solve each other's problems.

NETWORKS ARE THE ANSWER
John Naisbitt, author of *'Megatrends'* has predicted the rise of networks. He says that the usual corporate structure, a hierachy with rigid ranks and levels, is not conducive to human achievement. It makes it too hard to obtain information. Such an environment really works against the

concept of human achievement. In a heirarchy people sit on information and keep it to themselves.

Why? Because information is power and they do not want you to have power.

> ❖ *In a network, information is shared.*
> *This means that everyone has power.*

With power comes performance, and with performance come rewards - money growth and stability.

The modern network has no limits. It need not be restricted to operations within one company. For example, an estate agent in one company may find other estate agents in other cities, willing to share information. This is a network.

> *The power to achieve your goals can come from*
> *sharing information.*

NETWORKS ARE FOR ALL

Networks are not exclusive. There is only one rule:

If you can contribute, you can belong.

That is the great equaliser - your ability to help others in the system.

On both sides of the Atlantic there has always been an *old-boy-network*, based largely on ties from schooldays, university, clubs and societies. Such networks are both protective and insular. The networks of the 1990's and beyond will help people adapt to change - not fight it. People no longer have time for inefficient hierarchies and road blocks to information.

❖ *A study reported in 'Megatrends' stated that it takes seven phone calls to get information from a government department. In a network, members use 'connections' to cut through red tape and get the job done.*

NETWORKS & *MLM's*

A network is a perfect structure for an MLM. It is the co-operation between individuals that produces results. MLM's depend on networks - hence the term more often used in Britain, *Network Marketing.*

In an age where, through the relentless advance of technology, mental skills are more highly valued that physical skills, networking comes into its own, for it concentrates the mind. Finis Welch, a labour economist, discusses this concept in *Fortune* magazine (9/92). The networker looks ahead, identifies the problem and uses the help of others to overcome it.

In MLM, networkers have glimpsed the future and found it troubling, so they band together to solve the problems.

❖ *Network Marketing companies not only distribute products and services through networks - they pass information as well.*

There is a positive flow of information, in both directions. The company disseminates information to its distributors and receives feed-back from them.

This is two way communication at its very best.

Networks, like politics, are local. Each individual is at the centre of a network. In Network Marketing/MLM, distributors have up-lines and down-lines to help them achieve their goals.   This kind of natural co-operation between human beings is a rare commodity!

> ❖ *Imagine yourself succeeding in your most*
> *ambitious dreams, not by yourself,*
> *but in the company of people who really care about you.*

Please read that statement again.
It should hit you like a thunderclap.   A network is a family.
People who actually care about each other.

What would it mean to you to have some help?   Real help! When was the last time someone did some of your work?   Do you have neighbours, friends or members of your family that help you out - and that you help?

Can you visualise an entire business built with people helping one another?   Wouldn't you agree, that would be a fantastic thing?

In Network Marketing people help each other to distribute products - and they make a lot of money doing it. What is the first thing you notice when you attend a Network Marketing meeting?   People are happy - and not just for themselves, but for others.   When one person succeeds, everyone succeeds - and it happens all the time!

One of the greatest motivators to a human being is recognition - public recognition, as well as the recognition of their peers.   Network Marketing organisations often hold large conventions at which the performance of their distributors is publicly acknowledged by the presentation of awards.   Everyone receiving an award is making money. Why is everyone else clapping so enthusiastically?   *Because they are making money too.*

What would it take for you to get involved with a group of other people *who want you to make money?* Their enthusiasm - and that is what it is - is a totally genuine desire to see you succeed.

> ❖*Nobody stays in networking unless they are getting*
> *something out of it. For some people, it is recognition.*
> *For others it is increased income.*
> *For still others, it is a sense of belonging.*
> *For most though, it is the money - and all that it can bring.*

TO BUILD A NETWORK

Building a network is simple - if you have something worth bringing to it. It is something quite special and very valuable.

> ❖ *You become successful in Network Marketing*
> *WHEN YOU HELP OTHER PEOPLE*
> *TO REACH THEIR GOALS. Q.E.D*

That's what it takes to build a successful network. Help others to succeed. If you are in the right business, you will profit greatly from the success you build for other people.

You have something very special to share if you are in a Network Marketing business. You have opportunity - but that is only part of the equation. The people in your network must take advantage of the opportunity by applying themselves, and to do this, they will need your help.

And you will need the help of others. Your up-line will provide you with that help. And you in turn will help people in your down-line. This is your network at work.

GEOMETRIC PROGRESSION

A network works through geometric - or would it be more accurate to say *arithmetic* progression? Suppose you start a Network Marketing business with other people, offering them an opportunity. As long as they see the business as beneficial to them, they will join.

When they share the opportunity with other people, the business grows geometrically. For example, if you show 6 people how to create their own business, and they each share the business with 6 others, there are now 43 people in the business...

$$
\begin{array}{lcl}
\text{YOU} & = & 1 \\
\text{Your next 6 distributors} & = & 6 \\
\text{They each sponsor 6 distributors} & = & 36
\end{array}
$$

Total = 43

That is a geometric progression. You benefit from the total volume created.

Now suppose that you invest 10 hours per week in your business, and the people in your group also put 10 a week each into their business, 430 hours are being worked - and you benefit from all of them! Meanwhile you continue to put in just 10 hours of your own.

Now don't get the idea that *you are making money from* each of those distributors. Remember our chapter on distributors? Remember how tremendous quantities of money could be saved by shortening the distribution channel? Rather than spend money on salespeople, retailing overheads etc., the savings are given to the distributors. *This* is where the money comes from. The company sends you a bonus, based on the volume generated by your group. Everyone is rewarded according to their effort and performance. Each person shares in the profits of the company in direct ratio to the volume of their personal contribution.

> ❖ *It is free enterprise!*
> *Rewarding the people who produce, without taking anything out of the pockets of other people who are also producing - and all without any limitation on earnings!*

There are no employers withholding information and nobody worrying about the fact you may be earning more than them. In fact, your sponsor would be positively delighted if you made more than him!

You want people in your group to be wealthy, for if they are, you will be too. That is the beauty of networking - help others to reach their goals, and you cannot fail to reach yours!

SO WHAT DO YOU NEED TO DO?

This, of course, is the obvious question - or should be by now. You need to do something, and you need to do it right away.

DO IT NOW!

Start by making a commitment - to yourself, to your family, and eventually, to your own down-line. Find a Network Marketing company that fits your needs - *and stick with it.*

To be successful in a Network Marketing business you must be willing to make a six to nine month commitment to developing the distributive system on which your business is based. You must have a quality product or service, ideally a product which is consumable or replacable, that you believe in completely. Above all, you must be prepared to stick to your product and company and not be deviated from your purpose by the constant 'green-field' opportunities that will cross your path. That way you *will* succeed!

A QUESTION OF PRIORITIES

Why will you do this? Because your life has taken on new priorities. You are working hard now so that you will not have to later on. You are making choices now so that later you can make more exciting choices.

Don't fall back into the same old ruts. Give your life a jump start. Help others to succeed and you will have achieved the most worthwhile goals for yourself.

Imagine a life spent with successful people, working together with high ideals - does that sound like a progressive, rewarding life?

❖ *John Paul Getty in his book 'How to be rich', discusses six basic facts that govern success in business...*

- ■ *Own your own business*
- ■ *Market a product or service that is in great demand*
- ■ *Be sure the product is guaranteed*
- ■ *Give a better service than the competition*
- ■ *Reward and recognise those who do the work*
- ■ *Build your success upon the success of others*

Multi-level Marketing - Network Marketing is all of these things. Use your God-given talents, hold firmly onto your liberty, and seize the future. Here is an opportunity that is literally available to everyone -

It is truly becoming 'The People's Franchise'!

Original bibliography
(and further reading)

Administrative Science Quarterly
'The new owners: the mass emergence of employee ownership in public companies and what it means to American business' March 1993.

Advancing the American Dream Direct Selling Association.

Amagram 'The future is now' January 1990

The Atlanta Journal
'Who will hire me now?' August 29/1993

The Atlanta Journal
'A new captain takes the helm at Amway' August 1/1993

Business Opportunity July 1993

Business Tokyo 'Amway leads the way' November 1989

Business Week 'Work & family' June 28/1993

Business Week 'The information revolution' Spring 1994

Business Week
'Retailing will never be the same' July 26/1993

Business Week
'Why hit the middle class? That's where the money is.'
March 1/1993

Business Week
'Executive pay: Clinton curbs are out of touch - and out of bounds.' March 22/1993

Business Week
'What happened to the American Dream?' August 19/1991

Business Week
'Is interactive TV so much hype?' May 11/1993

Business Week
'Shopping by cable and phone.' November 2/1992

Business Week
'It's a lot tougher to mind the store' January 8/1990

Citrus County Chronicle
'Networks, not pyramids' February 21/1993

The Dentist
'Network Marketing: a profitable option' June 1992

Department of Health & Human Services Publication
'Heart attacks and Mondays' March 1991

<u>'Don't let anybody steal your dream'</u> Dexter R Yager Sr.1993

Forbes 'The death of the salesman' May 24/1993

Forbes
'The 400 largest private companies in the U.S.' Dec. 7/1992

Forbes 'The power of positive inspiration' December 9/1991

Forbes 'Soap and hope in Tokyo' September 3/1990

Fortune 'What's happening to jobs in America' July12/1993

Fortune 'A brave new Darwinian workplace' January 25/1993

Fortune
'How to protect your financial future' January 25/1993

Fortune
'Are strategic alliances working?' September 21/1992

Fortune 'Burned-out bosses' July 25/1994

Fortune 'Waking up to the new economy' June 27/1994

Fortune
'The truth about the rich and the poor' September 21/1992

'Goal setting' by Zig Ziglar. 1993

Harpers Magazine Average CEO earnings' September 1993

'How to be rich' by J.Paul Getty

Inbound Logistics 'A revolution's a'coming' April 1994

Income Opportunities
'10 top Network Marketing companies' September 1993

'Megatrends' by John Naisbitt 1982

'Multi Level Marketing' Nadler, Beverly

Nation's Business
'Selling American to the Japanese'   October 1990

National Underwriter
'Sweetening the pot for key execs.'   May 1993

<u>Network & Multi-Level Marketing</u>' by Allen Carmichael 1991

New business opportunities
'Step up to success...as Multilevel Marketing Cleans up its act'
October 1993

Newsweek   'There's still no free lunch'   April 12/1993

Newsweek   'Doctors under the knife'   April 5/1993

Ocala Star Banner
'Be your own boss with only hundreds of dollars'
November 28/1991

The Orlando Sentinel
'Magazine flushes out tough bosses'   September 29/1993

The Orlando Sentinel
'Spiegel unwraps retail channels'   September 28/1993

The Orlando Sentinel
'Cutbacks not always best option'   September 16/1993

The Orlando Sentinel
'Worker's priorities undergo upheaval'   September 15/1993
Pennsylvania Hospitals Nineties

'Futurist predicts collaboration holds promise for healthier future' August 2/1993

The Reporter 'Workers in gridlock' September 6/1993

Review of Social Economy
'Smith's view on human nature: a problem in the interpretation' 1977

Success 'Global paradox' March 1994

Success 'The greatest motivator' December 1993

Success 'Unlimited wealth' October 1993

Success 'Unlimited future' September 1993

Success 'Charismatic capitalism' May 1993

Success 'The $4-billion man' May 1993

Success 'The mindset of the rich' March 1993

Success 'Look before you leap' January/February 1993

Success 'Magic marketing' March 1992

Success 'We create millionaires' March 1992

Success 'The new feudalism' January 1992

Success 'Network Marketing' May 1990

U.S. Department of Labor 'What work requires of schools'

U.S. News & World Report
'White collar wasteland' June 28/1993

U.S. News & World Report
'On the wrong track' May 10/1993

<u>'Unlimited Wealth'</u> by Paul Zane Pilzer

Upline 'Network Marketing and the American Dream'
March 1993

USA Today
'Many in 50's face hard years' June 18-20/1993

The Wall Street Journal
'Hungarians seeking to find a new way find instead Amway'
January 15/1993

The Wall Street Journal
'Wal-Mart set to eliminate reps, brokers' December 2/1991

<u>'Who stole the American Dream?'</u> by Burke Hedges 1992

Your Next Move (Internet Services Corporation)
'The price of success' 1990

APPENDIX - *Goal setting*

You cannot hope to achieve your objectives unless you know what they are! This is your opportunity to really think about the things that are important to you, especially related to your journey towards financial security.

As with all journeys into unknown territory, a map is vital since it not only shows you how to reach your goal, it also enables you to see how far you still have to travel, and how far you have already come.

Goal setting, once you have decided on your priorities, is easy - but a plan is needed to map the route.

Within the covers of this book you will find that plan.

Start your goal setting by making a list of the things you want for yourself and for your family, the things you would dearly like to achieve. The list should include:

- the sort of home you would like
- ideally, where you would like it to be
- the car you would like to drive
- the date by which you would like to be free of all debts
- the type of education you would like for your children
- the date by which you would like to retire
- the help you would like to give to others
- the charities you would like to support
  etc.,etc

Flesh out your list with plenty of detail, being as specific as possible. Really pin down your dreams! If you can find photographs of say, the type of house, the model and make of car, paste them beside your list. But, above all, *put dates beside each item* indicating a time scale for its achievement. That is particularly important.

By completing this exercise you are clearly establishing your future. Keep this list handy and read through it from time to time. Add to it, if other goals come to mind - but always tie them down with a date. Remember...

...success is a journey, not a destination.

GOAL SETTING

*The following pages are reserved for goal setting.
Remember, it is important to be as specific as possible.
We suggest you use one page for each goal.*

GOAL SETTING (2)

GOAL SETTING (3)

GOAL SETTING (4)

GOAL SETTING (5)

GOAL SETTING (6)

GOAL SETTING (7)

GOAL SETTING (8)